Where Do We Live

Published by Methuen 2002

1 3 5 7 9 10 8 6 4 2

First published in Great Britain in 2002
by Methuen Publishing Limited,
215 Vauxhall Bridge Road, London SW1V 1EJ

Copyright © 2002 Christopher Shinn

The author has asserted his rights under the Copyright, Designs
and Patents Act, 1988, to be identified as the author of this work

Methuen Publishing Limited Reg. No. 3543167

A CIP catalogue record for this book
is available from the British Library

ISBN 0 413 77272 1

Typeset by MATS, Southend-on-Sea, Essex

Printed and bound in Great Britain by
Cox & Wyman Ltd, Reading, Berkshire

Caution

ROYAL COURT

Royal Court Theatre presents

WHERE DO WE LIVE

by **Christopher Shinn**

First performance at the Royal Court Jerwood Theatre Upstairs
Sloane Square, London on 17 May 2002.

Supported by the American Friends of the Royal Court Theatre.

WHERE DO WE LIVE

by **Christopher Shinn**

Cast in alphabetical order
Dave/Young White Guy/Young White Man/Young Business Man 1
Nicholas Aaron
Shedrick **Noel Clarke**
Billy/Young Business Man 2/Art Student **Toby Dantzic**
Stephen **Daniel Evans**
Tyler **Adam Garcia**
Timothy **Cyril Nri**
Leo/Violinist **Ray Panthaki**
Lily **Jemima Rooper**
Patricia **Susannah Wise**

Director **Richard Wilson**
Designer **Julian McGowan**
Lighting Designer **Johanna Town**
Sound Designer **Paul Arditti**
Composer **Olly Fox**
Assistant Director **Tim Roseman**
Casting Director **Lisa Makin**
Production Manager **Sue Bird**
Company Stage Manager **Cath Binks**
Stage Management **Pea Horsley, Emily Danby**
Stage Management Work Placement **Graeme Brown**
Costume Supervisor **Laura Hunt**
Wardrobe Mistress **Jackie Orton**
Dialect Coach **Joan Washington**
Company Voice Work **Patsy Rodenburg**

Royal Court Theatre would like to thank the following for their help with this production:
Mr Shinn's travel and accomodation in London was made possible by the Laura Pels Foundation.
Oberon Books, Camden Education Department, connectinglondon.com, Acclaim Entertainment, Chelsea
& Westminster Hospital. Wardrobe care by Persil and Comfort courtesy of Lever Fabergé.

THE COMPANY

Christopher Shinn (writer)
For the Royal Court: Other People, Four.
Other theatre includes: The Coming World (Soho).

Nicholas Aaron
Theatre includes: Badfinger (Grand Theatre
Swansea); Sparkleshark (RNT).
Television includes: Dirty Work, Band of Brothers,
Fun at the Funeral, Parlour, The Bench.
Film includes: The Initiation of Samuel Caine, Killing
Me Softly, Lemmings, Don't Look Back.

Paul Arditti (sound designer)
Paul Arditti has been designing sound for theatre
since 1983, including over 70 shows for the Royal
Court.
Productions for the Royal Court include: The Night
Heron, Plasticine, Boy Gets Girl, Clubland, Blasted,
Mouth To Mouth, Spinning Into Butter, I Just
Stopped By To See The Man, Far Away, My Zinc
Bed, 4.48 Psychosis, Fireface, Mr Kolpert, The
Force of Change, Other People, Dublin Carol, The
Glory of Living, The Kitchen, Rat in the Skull, Some
Voices, Mojo, The Weir; The Steward of
Christendom, Shopping and Fucking, Blue Heart
(co-productions with Out of Joint); The Chairs (co-
production with Theatre de Complicite); Cleansed,
Via Dolorosa.
Other theatre includes: Hinterland (Out of Joint);
Afore Night Come (Young Vic); Tales From
Hollywood (Donmar); Light (Complicite); Our Lady
of Sligo (RNT with Out of Joint); Some Explicit
Polaroids (Out of Joint); Hamlet, The Tempest
(RSC); Orpheus Descending, Cyrano de Bergerac,
St Joan (West End); Marathon (Gate).
Musicals include: Doctor Dolittle, Piaf, The
Threepenny Opera.
Awards include: Drama Desk Award for
Outstanding Sound Design 1992 for Four Baboons
Adoring the Sun (Broadway).

Noel Clarke
Theatre includes: Talking About Men (Oval).
Television includes: Auf Weidersehen Pet, Casualty,
Waking the Dead, Metrosexuality, Judge John Deed,
The Bill.
Film includes: Take 2, Native Saramar,
Hetrosexuality Vicarious.
Radio includes: Soldier Boy.

Toby Dantzic
Theatre includes: The Misanthrope (Chichester
Festival Theatre).

Daniel Evans
For the Royal Court: 4.48 Psychosis, Other
People, Cleansed.
Other theatre includes: Ghosts (English
Touring Theatre); Merrily We Roll Along
(Donmar Warehouse), Candide, The
Merchant of Venice, Troilus & Cressida, Peter
Pan, Cardiff East (RNT); Henry V, Coriolanus,
A Midsummer Night's Dream (RSC).
Television includes: Helen West, Being Dom
Joly, Trigger Happy TV, Love In A Cold
Climate, The Vice, Deep Sleep, Great
Expectations, The Case of the Private Spiers,
Be Brave, Soldier, Soldier, Nel, As You Like It,
Romeo and Juliet.
Film includes: Sweeney, The Barber of Siberia,
Chameleon, A Midsummer Night's Dream,
Mabinogi.
Radio includes: War and Peace, Wuthering
Heights, Gymerwch Chi Sigaret?
Awards include: Olivier nomination for
Candide, Olivier Award for Best Actor in a
Musical for Merrily We Roll Along (2001).

Olly Fox (composer)
For the Royal Court: Mr Kolpert.
Other theatre includes: Bones (Hampstead),
Hand in Hand (sound design, Hampstead);
The Duchess of Malfi, Macbeth, Equus, The
Winter's Tale (Salisbury Playhouse); The
Caretaker (English Touring Theatre), The
Good Woman of Szechuan (RNT); The Three
Birds (Gate); The Way of the World, Eliza's
House, Two Clouds Over Eden (Royal
Exchange, Manchester); Cold (Ashton
Contemporary Theatre Group); See-Saw
(Quarantine at The Tramway, Glasgow); The
Taming of the Shrew (English Touring
Theatre); Lifegame (Improbable Theatre at
Lyric, Hammersmith & national tour); But the
Living Are Wrong in the Sharp Distinctions
They Make, The Wasp Factory (Northern
Stage); Mother Courage, A Midsummer
Night's Dream, The Mill on the Floss
(Contact). Olly has also written songs and
scores for other productions at The Young Vic
Studio, The Unicorn Theatre for Children,
Live Theatre, Newcastle, BAC, Walk The
Plank, Spare Tyre, New Writing North, ENO
Bayliss Programme.
Television includes: The Royal Collection
(BBC).
Radio includes: Millport (series 2); Through
the Looking Glass, The Ghost of Federico
Garcia Lorca, Wainwright The Poisoner, The
Echoing Waters, Desire Lines (BBC).

Adam Garcia

Theatre includes: Cadillac Ranch (Soho); Saturday Night Fever (London Palladium); Birdy (Comedy Theatre/Lyric, Hammersmith); Grease (Dominion); Hot Shoe Shuffle (Queens). Television includes: Dream Team, Wild House. Film includes: The First 20 Million Is Always the Hardest, Riding In Cars With Boys, Coyote Ugly, Bootmen, Wilde.

Awards includes: Olivier Award Nomination for Best Actor in a Musical for Saturday Night Fever.

Julian McGowan (designer)

For the Royal Court: Sliding With Suzanne (co-production with Out of Joint), I Just Stopped By to See the Man, Mr Kolpert, Toast, The Censor, Shopping and Fucking (co-production with Out of Joint), American Bagpipes, The Treatment; The Steward of Christendom, Blue Heart (with Out of Joint).

Other theatre includes: Feelgood (Garrick); Four Nights at Knaresborough (New Vic Workshop at the Tricycle), Enjoy, Blast From the Past, Tess of the D'Urbevilles (West Yorkshire Playhouse); Some Explicit Polaroids (Out of Joint); Waiting for Godot, Don Juan, The Lodger, Women Laughing (Royal Exchange, Manchester); Our Lady of Sligo (Out of Joint/RNT); Our Country's Good (Out of Joint/Young Vic); The Positive Hour (Out of Joint/Hampstead); The Possibilities, Venice Preserv'd, The LA Plays (Almeida); Heart Throb (Bush); The Wives' Excuse (Royal Shakespeare Company); Caesar and Cleopatra, Total Eclipse, A Tale of Two Cities (Greenwich); The Rivals, Man and Superman, Playboy of the Western World, Hedda Gabler.

Opera includes: Cosi Fan Tutte (New Israeli Opera); Eugene Onegin (Scottish Opera); Siren Song (Almeida Opera Festival).

Cyril Nri

For the Royal Court: Search and Destroy, Ficky Stingers, A Colder Climate, Prairie Du Chien, Edmond.

Other theatre includes: The Darker Face of the Earth, The Way of The World, Blood Wedding (RNT); Playboy of the West Indies, The Piano Lesson, All or Nothing (Tricycle); Road (Cochrane Theatre); The Dragon Can't Dance (Stratford East); Desire (Almeida); Macbeth (RNT/American tour); The Tempest (Old Vic); Serious Money (Wyndhams); The Price of Experience (Traverse); Ridley Walker, Class K, Great Expectations (Royal Exchange); Oedipus Rex (Contact); Kiss Me Kate, Breaking The Ice, Life's A Dream, Volpone, Henry VIII, Twelfth Night, Julius Caeser (RSC).

Television includes: Down To Earth II, Doctors III, Eastenders, Holby City, Family Affairs, Arabian Nights, Maisie Raine II, A Touch Of Frost, Only Love, Goodnight Sweetheart, This Life, Pie In The Sky, Casualty, Frank Stubbs Promotes, Calling The Shots, A Strike Out of Time, Saracen, The Bill.

Film includes: Long Time Dead, Beseiged, Talos the Mummy, The Steal, King of Jazz, Strapless, Borderland.

Ray Panthaki

Television includes: Spooks, Rehab, My Family, Blood Strangers, Armando Ianucci Show, Losing It, The Bill.

Film includes: 28 Days Later, Bollywood Queen, A To Z, Ali-G Indahouse, Tube Tales, Z, Extra Time, Jump Boy.

Jemima Rooper

For the Royal Court: Workers Writes (Royal Court Young Writers Programme).

Other theatre includes: Oscar (King's Head, Islington).

Television includes: As If, Love in a Cold Climate, Urban Gothic, The Railway Children, Dance, Lifeforce, Summer in the Suburbs, Wives and Daughters, The Passion, Junk, Animal Ark, The Famous Five.

Film includes: Hermit of Amsterdam, Owd Bob, Willy's War, The Higher Mortals.

Tim Roseman (assistant director)

As assistant director theatre includes: Conversations After a Burial (Almeida).

As director theatre includes: Cosí (New End & Australian High Commission); Lovers (New End); 90 Minutes (Southwark Playhouse); Karen Morris Gala (Old Vic); Nearly All Sondheim (Greenwich Playhouse); Kingdom on Earth (Landor); The Seagull/The Cherry Orchard, Love for Love, The Good Person of Szechuan, The Women of Troy (Academy of Live and Recorded Arts).

Tim has directed readings at the Young Vic and Old Vic.

Tim's work on this production is supported by the Channel Four/Royal Court Drama Directors Programme.

Johanna Town (lighting designer)
Johanna has been Head of Lighting for the Royal Court since 1990 and has designed extensively for the company during this time.
Productions include: Plasticine, Fucking Games, Nightingale and Chase, Sliding With Suzanne (co-production with Out of Joint), I Just Stopped By To See The Man, Under the Blue Sky, Mr Kolpert, Other People, Toast, The Kitchen, Faith Healer, Pale Horse, Search and Destroy.
Other recent theatre designs include: She Stoops To Conquer (Kent Opera); Hinterland (Out of Joint/RNT); Top Girls (Aldwych/West End/OSC); Les Liaison Dangereuses (Liverpool Playhouse); Feelgood (Out of Joint/ Hampstead/ Garrick); Playboy of the Western World (Liverpool Playhouse); Rita, Sue and Bob Too, A State Affair (Out of Joint/Soho Theatre); Arabian Nights (New Victory, New York); Our Lady of Sligo (Irish Repertory Theatre, New York); Rose (RNT/ Broadway); Little Malcolm (Hampstead/ West End); Blue Heart (Royal Court/Out of Joint/ New York); Tobias and the Angel (Almeida Opera Festival).

Richard Wilson (director)
Associate Director of the Royal Court.
For the Royal Court: Nightingale and Chase, I Just Stopped By To See The Man, Mr Kolpert (for which he won the TMA Award for Best Theatre Director), Toast, Four, God's Second in Command, Other Worlds, Heaven and Hell; A Wholly Healthy Glasgow, Women Laughing (both originally at the Royal Exchange, Manchester).
Other theatre includes: Four Knights in Knaresborough (New Vic Workshop for Tricycle); Tom & Clem (tour and West End); Simply Disconnected (Chichester); The Lodger (Hampstead /Royal Exchange, Manchester); Imagine Drowning, President Wilson in Paris, Lenz (Hampstead); Prin (Lyric Hammersmith); An Inspector Calls (Royal Exchange, Manchester); View of Kabul, Commitments (Bush); Teeth 'n' Smiles (Oxford Playhouse).
Television includes: Changing Step, A Wholly Healthy Glasgow, Under The Hammer, Remainder Man, Commitments.
Richard Wilson has many other credits for theatre, film and television as both an actor and a director.

Susannah Wise
Theatre includes: Life After George (West End); Three Sisters, Heartbreak House (Chichester Festival Theatre); The Critic, The Dispute, The Candidate (Royal Exchange, Manchester); Golem (National Studio); Hay Fever (Crucible, Sheffield); Featuring Loretta (Hampstead); The Prime of Miss Jean Brodie (RNT).
Television includes: The Strawberry Tree, As You Like It Rehearsal, A Nice Cup Of Tea, Class Act, Casualty, Bliss, Eskimo Day, The Bill, Dalziel & Pascoe, The Tenant of Wildfell Hall, Staying Alive, Where The Heart Is, Faith In The Future, In A Land Of Plenty, Kavanagh QC.
Film includes: An Ideal Husband, Britannic.

THE ENGLISH STAGE COMPANY AT THE ROYAL COURT

The English Stage Company at the Royal Court opened in 1956 as a subsidised theatre producing new British plays, international plays and some classical revivals.

The first artistic director George Devine aimed to create a writers' theatre, 'a place where the dramatist is acknowledged as the fundamental creative force in the theatre and where the play is more important than the actors, the director, the designer'. The urgent need was to find a contemporary style in which the play, the acting, direction and design are all combined. He believed that 'the battle will be a long one to continue to create the right conditions for writers to work in'.

Devine aimed to discover 'hard-hitting, uncompromising writers whose plays are stimulating, provocative and exciting'. The Royal Court production of John Osborne's Look Back in Anger in May 1956 is now seen as the decisive starting point of modern British drama and the policy created a new generation of British playwrights. The first wave included John Osborne, Arnold Wesker, John Arden, Ann Jellicoe, N F Simpson and Edward Bond. Early seasons included new international plays by Bertolt Brecht, Eugène Ionesco, Samuel Beckett, Jean-Paul Sartre and Marguerite Duras.

The theatre started with the 400-seat proscenium arch Theatre Downstairs, and then in 1969 opened a second theatre, the 60-seat studio Theatre Upstairs. Some productions transfer to the West End, such as Caryl Churchill's Far Away, Conor McPherson's The Weir, Kevin Elyot's Mouth to Mouth and My Night With Reg. The Royal Court also co-produces plays which have transferred to the West End or toured internationally, such as Sebastian Barry's The Steward of Christendom and Mark Ravenhill's Shopping and Fucking (with Out of Joint), Martin McDonagh's The Beauty Queen Of Leenane (with Druid Theatre Company), Ayub Khan-Din's East is East (with Tamasha Theatre Company, and now a feature film).

Since 1994 the Royal Court's artistic policy has again been vigorously directed to finding and producing a new generation of playwrights. The writers include Joe Penhall, Rebecca Prichard, Michael Wynne, Nick Grosso, Judy Upton, Meredith Oakes, Sarah Kane, Anthony Neilson, Judith Johnson, James Stock, Jez Butterworth, Marina Carr, Simon Block, Martin McDonagh, Mark Ravenhill, Ayub Khan-Din, Tamantha Hammerschlag, Jess Walters, Che Walker, Conor McPherson, Simon Stephens, Richard Bean, Roy

photo: Andy Chopping

Williams, Gary Mitchell, Mick Mahoney, Rebecca Gilman, Christopher Shinn, Kia Corthron, David Gieselmann, Marius von Mayenburg, David Eldridge, Leo Butler, Zinnie Harris, Grae Cleugh, Roland Schimmelpfennig and Vassily Sigarev. This expanded programme of new plays has been made possible through the support of A.S.K Theater Projects, the Jerwood Charitable Foundation, the American Friends of the Royal Court Theatre and many in association with the Royal National Theatre Studio.

In recent years there have been record-breaking productions at the box office, with capacity houses for Rebecca Gilman's Boy Gets Girl, Kevin Elyot's Mouth To Mouth, David Hare's My Zinc Bed and Conor McPherson's The Weir, which transferred to the West End in October 1998 and ran for nearly two years at the Duke of York's Theatre.

The newly refurbished theatre in Sloane Square opened in February 2000, with a policy still inspired by the first artistic director George Devine. The Royal Court is an international theatre for new plays and new playwrights, and the work shapes contemporary drama in Britain and overseas.

REBUILDING THE ROYAL COURT

In 1995, the Royal Court was awarded a National Lottery grant through the Arts Council of England, to pay for three quarters of a £26m project to completely rebuild its 100-year old home. The rules of the award required the Royal Court to raise £7.6m in partnership funding. The building has been completed thanks to the generous support of those listed below.

We are particularly grateful for the contributions of over 5,700 audience members.

English Stage Company Registered Charity number 231242.

THE AMERICAN FRIENDS OF THE ROYAL COURT THEATRE

AFRCT support the mission of the Royal Court and are primarily focused on raising funds to enable the theatre to produce new work by emerging American writers. Since this not-for-profit organisation was founded in 1997, AFRCT has contributed to eight productions including Christopher Shinn's Where Do We Live They have also supported the participation of young artists in the Royal Court's acclaimed International Residency.

If you would like to support the ongoing work of the Royal Court, please contact the Development Department on 020 7565 5050.

THE ARTS COUNCIL OF ENGLAND

PROGRAMME SUPPORTERS

The Royal Court (English Stage Company Ltd) receives its principal funding from London Arts. It is also supported financially by a wide range of private companies and public bodies and earns the remainder of its income from the box office and its own trading activities.

The Royal Borough of Kensington & Chelsea gives an annual grant to the Royal Court Young Writers' Programme and the Affiliation of London Government provides project funding for a number of play development initiatives.

The Jerwood Charitable Foundation continues to support new plays by new playwrights through the Jerwood New Playwrights series. Since 1993 the A.S.K. Theater Projects of Los Angeles has funded a Playwrights' Programme at the theatre. Bloomberg Mondays, the Royal Court's reduced price ticket scheme, is supported by Bloomberg.

Over the past seven years the BBC has supported the Gerald Chapman Fund for directors.

London Government   LONDON ARTS

AWARDS FOR
THE ROYAL COURT

Terry Johnson's Hysteria won the 1994 Olivier Award for Best Comedy, and also the Writers' Guild Award for Best West End Play. Kevin Elyot's My Night with Reg won the 1994 Writers' Guild Award for Best Fringe Play, the Evening Standard Award for Best Comedy, and the 1994 Olivier Award for Best Comedy. Joe Penhall was joint winner of the 1994 John Whiting Award for Some Voices. Sebastian Barry won the 1995 Writers' Guild Award for Best Fringe Play, the Critics' Circle Award and the 1995 Lloyds Private Banking Playwright of the Year Award for The Steward of Christendom. Jez Butterworth won the 1995 George Devine Award, the Writers' Guild New Writer of the Year Award, the Evening Standard Award for Most Promising Playwright and the Olivier Award for Best Comedy for Mojo.

The Royal Court was the overall winner of the 1995 Prudential Award for the Arts for creativity, excellence, innovation and accessibility. The Royal Court Theatre Upstairs won the 1995 Peter Brook Empty Space Award for innovation and excellence in theatre.

Michael Wynne won the 1996 Meyer-Whitworth Award for The Knocky. Martin McDonagh won the 1996 George Devine Award, the 1996 Writers' Guild Best Fringe Play Award, the 1996 Critics' Circle Award and the 1996 Evening Standard Award for Most Promising Playwright for The Beauty Queen of Leenane. Marina Carr won the 19th Susan Smith Blackburn Prize (1996/7) for Portia Coughlan. Conor McPherson won the 1997 George Devine Award, the 1997 Critics' Circle Award and the 1997 Evening Standard Award for Most Promising Playwright for The Weir. Ayub Khan-Din won the 1997 Writers' Guild Awards for Best West End Play and Writers' Guild New Writer of the Year and the 1996 John Whiting Award for East is East (co-production with Tamasha).

At the 1998 Tony Awards, Martin McDonagh's The Beauty Queen of Leenane (co-production with Druid Theatre Company) won four awards including Garry Hynes for Best Director and was nominated for a further two. Eugene Ionesco's The Chairs (co-production with Theatre de Complicite) was nominated for six Tony awards. David Hare won the 1998 Time Out Live Award for Outstanding Achievement and six awards in New York including the Drama League, Drama Desk and New York Critics Circle Award for Via Dolorosa. Sarah Kane won the 1998 Arts Foundation Fellowship in Playwriting. Rebecca Prichard won the 1998 Critics' Circle Award for Most Promising Playwright for Yard Gal (co-production with Clean Break).

Conor McPherson won the 1999 Olivier Award for Best New Play for The Weir. The Royal Court won the 1999 ITI Award for Excellence in International Theatre. Sarah Kane's Cleansed was judged Best Foreign Language Play in 1999 by Theater Heute in Germany. Gary Mitchell won the 1999 Pearson Best Play Award for Trust. Rebecca Gilman was joint winner of the 1999 George Devine Award and won the 1999 Evening Standard Award for Most Promising Playwright for The Glory of Living.

Roy Williams and Gary Mitchell were joint winners of the George Devine Award 2000 for Most Promising Playwright for Lift Off and The Force of Change respectively. At the Barclays Theatre Awards 2000 presented by the TMA, Richard Wilson won the Best Director Award for David Gieselmann's Mr Kolpert and Jeremy Herbert won the Best Designer Award for Sarah Kane's 4.48 Psychosis. Gary Mitchell won the Evening Standard's Charles Wintour Award 2000 for Most Promising Playwright for The Force of Change. Stephen Jeffreys' I Just Stopped by to See The Man won an AT&T: On Stage Award 2000. David Eldridge's Under the Blue Sky won the Time Out Live Award 2001 for Best New Play in the West End. Leo Butler won the George Devine Award 2001 for Most Promising Playwright for Redundant. Roy Williams won the Evening Standard's Charles Wintour Award 2001 for Most Promising Playwright for Clubland. Grae Cleugh won the 2001 Olivier Award for Most Promising Playwright for Fucking Games.

In 1999, the Royal Court won the European theatre prize New Theatrical Realities, presented at Taormina Arte in Sicily, for its efforts in recent years in discovering and producing the work of young British dramatists.

ROYAL COURT BOOKSHOP

The bookshop offers a wide range of playtexts and theatre books, with over 1,000 titles. Located in the downstairs Bar and Food area, the bookshop is open Monday to Saturday, afternoons and evenings.

Many Royal Court playtexts are available for just £2 including works by Harold Pinter, Caryl Churchill, Rebecca Gilman, Martin Crimp, Sarah Kane, Conor McPherson, Ayub Khan-Din, Timberlake Wertenbaker and Roy Williams.

For information on titles and special events, Email: bookshop@royalcourttheatre.com
Tel: 020 7565 5024

Where Do We Live

Characters

Stephen, *late twenties, white*
Patricia, *late twenties, white*
Tyler, *late twenties, white*
Billy, *late twenties, white*
Shed, *early twenties, black*
Timothy, *early forties, black*
Lily, *mid-twenties, white*
Dave, *late teens, white*
Leo, *mid-twenties, Asian*
Young White Guy, *mid-twenties, white*
Young White Man, *late twenties, white*
Young Businessman 1, *late twenties, white*
Young Businessman 2, *late twenties, white*
Security Guard, *early forties, black*
Violinist, *mid-twenties, Asian*
Young Art Student, *mid-twenties, white*

Time: as indicated.

Place: New York City.

Note

The play may be performed by nine actors. The actor who
plays Dave may play Young White Guy, Young White Man
and Young Businessman 1; the actor who plays Billy may play
Young Businessman 2 and Young Art Student; the actor who
plays Leo may play the Violinist; and the actor who plays
Timothy may play the Security Guard.

I suspect the play's design should be simple and allow for
seamless transitions; be indicative rather than representative.
An insistent urban space with clear but weak boundaries,
where different worlds press hard against each other, bleed
through, blend and bend.

Interval follows Scene Six.

Acknowledgements

I would like to thank, for their generosity in aiding the
development of this play: John Buzzetti, Graham Whybrow,
Dominic Cooke, Daniel Evans, James Frain, Richard Wilson,
Doraly Rosen, Tim Farrell, John Belluso, Stuart Spencer,
Zach Shaffer, Gregory Mosher, Sarah Schuhman, David
Greenspan, Armando Riesco, Carmelo Larose and Keith
Nobbs.

For Kent Rees and Francine Volpe

Prologue

Slide: July 28, 2001.

A bar. **Patricia** *works behind the bar.* **Stephen** *sits, with soda.*
Two Young Businessmen *sit a few stools away, looking up at*
stock quotes on the television.

Stephen   And he said, 'Ooh, you don't want to be a
caretaker.'

Patricia   Oh. Of course.

Stephen   And I thought – I mean, the guy's missing a *leg*,
what? . . .

Patricia   Of course you did.

Stephen   And he knew the facts.

Patricia   What are the facts?

Patricia *listens while filling pretzel bowls.*

Stephen   Well. When I moved in, I just noticed – a family.
There was a woman – and there was a man – and a kid –
maybe eighteen. So one day the woman dies – I assume she
dies because I saw the kid – you know, he's in baggy pants,
basketball jersey – he's on the floor outside the apartment,
crying. And I never saw the woman after this day, so I assume
she/died.

Young Businessman 1   One more round here, Patricia.

Patricia *pours two whiskeys.*

Patricia (*nodding to TV, pouring drinks*)   You guys losing
money today?

Young Businessman 2   You're a loser if you're
losing/money.

Young Businessman 1   You gotta be crazy to lose money
in this market.

Young Businessman 2 (*nodding towards* **Stephen**)   What's
your boyfriend's name?

Patricia (*laughs, gives whiskeys to men*)   Here you go.

She *goes back to* **Stephen**, *keeps refilling pretzel bowls*.

So she dies.

Stephen   – I assume. And the, the man, the older man, he has no leg suddenly. I see him, he has no leg below the knee.

Bar phone rings. **Patricia** *answers.*

Patricia   Hello?

Young Businessman 1 (*to* **Patricia**)   Ah, *that's* your boyfriend.

Young Businessman 2 (*to* **Stephen**)   She have a boyfriend? She never tells us.

Patricia   Okay

Patricia *hangs up.*

Young Businessman 2   You ready to invest yet, Patricia?

Patricia   I'm already in the stock market – it goes up, I get good tips, if it goes down I know it's gonna be a bad day.

Young Businessman 1   You're lucky Bush got in.

Patricia   Right, yeah, thank God.

Young Businessman 1   More money for you!

Young Businessman 2   Three-hundred-dollar tax refund, what is that, how many tips is that? How many drinks you have to serve to get that?

Patricia goes back to **Stephen**. The **Businessmen** *laugh*.

Patricia   Okay, so.

Stephen   Anyway – so the mom dies, the dad loses his leg, and I can't tell for sure but I think the kid, I think the kid is dealing drugs out of the apartment, because I see people go in there during the day – white people – so that's the situation basically.

Young Businessman 1 (*re: the TV*)   Bingo. I told/you.

Young Businessman 2   Yeah, yeah, it'll drop, just/watch.

Young Businessman 1   I don't/think so.

Stephen   Anyway – the guy, the father – asks me for cigarettes – knocks on my door maybe once a week and asks. This has never seemed to bother Tyler – *until*. The other night.

The phone rings. **Patricia** *answers it.*

Patricia   Hello?

Young Businessman 2 (*to* **Stephen**)   What do you do?

Stephen   I'm a writer.

Young Businessman 1   Oh, yeah? A screenwriter?

Stephen   No, not a/screenwriter.

Young Businessman 2   You should write a story about us. I'm/serious.

Young Businessman 1   Yeah, this guy's life is screwed up, let me/tell you.

Young Businessman 2   – Two guys, one of them gets laid all the time, the other one can't/get laid.

Stephen (*amiably*)   Maybe I will.

Patricia   Okay, gotcha.

She hangs up and goes to **Stephen**. *Starts drying glasses.*

The other night.

Stephen   The other night. The guy knocks on my door. He needs to go to the deli. It's raining outside and he's afraid his crutches will slip. He tells me if he falls on his leg – the amputated leg, the remaining part of it – he'll be in really bad trouble. So I help him – I go with him – to the deli. And as we're walking, he starts talking. Telling me he's worked his whole life, he can't work anymore, he's on social security. He says, 'I tell him I'll give him five dollars to go down and get me cigarettes, but he doesn't do it, I get no help in there.' So – he buys some cheese and some cigarettes – and I'm thinking, Christ, there *must* be cigarettes in this apartment, how – how is this man living? Anyway – so I tell Tyler about this, I tell him this, and his response is – and this is his *instinctive* response – 'Oooh, be careful, you don't want to become a caretaker.'

Patricia   I see. Do you love this person?

Stephen   Do I love him? Yeah – yeah. I do. I really/do.

His cellphone rings. He checks the number, answers.

Hey, sweets. Nothing, just stopped by to see Patricia. Yeah? Okay. Okay, great. Bye.

He hangs up.

Patricia   It's funny – because from what you've told me about him, he's been taken care of.

Stephen   What?

Patricia   Was that him, by the way?

Stephen   Yeah.

Patricia   You told me that he has a trust fund. He's never had to worry about money.

Stephen   Right.

Patricia   He's been taken care of. So why was he threatened by your taking care of someone?

Stephen   Right – It made me think about empathy.

Patricia *clears* **Stephen's** *empty soda, wipes down the bar.*

Patricia   Uh-huh?

Stephen   Just – what it is. How it comes to be. On an individual level, a societal level . . . how do you imagine other people, their lives – whether it's someone you love or someone you don't – a stranger. – I should get going, we're 'clubbing' tonight. – I guess it's really a small thing to get so worked up about.

Patricia No it's not. (*Beat.*) I mean – the way you spoke of it, it doesn't sound like a small thing to you.

Pause.

Stephen (*lightly*) Yeah. Okay. I'll see you soon.

Stephen *puts down money for his soda.*

Patricia Shut up.

Stephen *laughs and takes his money back, goes, off.*

Young Businessman 1 (*to* **Patricia**) Blah blah blah, *Jesus*, that guy can talk. – Is he gay, that guy?

Patricia (*teasingly*) What do you think?

Young Businessman 2 (*to* **Young Businessman 1**) I told you he was.

Young Businessman 1 He's a writer like you,/huh?

Young Businessman 2 – You know, Patricia, there's this whole trend of attractive women hanging around gay guys, I saw a thing about it on TV.

Patricia (*laughing*) Is that so? This is a trend now?

The men rise, take out money, preparing to go.

Young Businessman 2 Yeah, but it's not healthy, they're afraid of real men, they've been hurt too many times, so they take comfort in gay men. But it's bad, you're/cutting off from –

Young Businessman 1 Don't listen to this/guy, Patricia.

Young Businessman 2 What? It's just an/observation.

Patricia I actually have a boyfriend, but thank you for your concern.

Young Businessman 2   You *do*. Truth is out. – That's a lucky guy. What's his name?

Patricia   Frank.

Young Businessman 2   What's he do?

Patricia   He's a chef.

Young Businessman 2   A chef? What kind of money do chefs make?

Young Businessman 1 (*Starting to go*)   We'll get out of your hair, Patricia.

Patricia (*laughing*)   Take care, you guys.

Young Businessman 1   But I'm serious, Patricia, you'll be voting Republican by the time we're through with you.

Patricia   Yeah, right.

Young Businessman 2 (*going*)   Hey, whenever you're ready to invest some money, you talk to me first, okay?

Patricia   Gotcha.

'I wish to examine the place, using the word in an abstract sense, where we most of the time are when we are experiencing life . . . If we look at our lives we shall probably find that we spend most of our time neither in behaviour nor in contemplation, but somewhere else. I ask: where? And I try to suggest an answer.'

– D.W. Winnicott, *Playing and Reality*

Act One

Scene One

Stephen's apartment. R & B music plays. **Stephen** *is dressing. A knock on his apartment door.* **Stephen** *turns down music and opens the door.*

Young White Guy   Your elevator is *scary, yo*!

Stephen   Sorry?

Young White Guy   The elevator is so old!

Stephen   I'm not – sure/what –

Young White Guy   Oh, fuck – have the wrong apartment.

Stephen   Oh.

Young White Guy   Sorry!

Stephen   That's o*kay*.

He shuts the door. He begins dressing and singing and dancing as he does. There is another knock on the door. He goes to the peephole and looks in.

Hello?

Shed's voice   Yeah, open up a minute?

Stephen   I'm sorry, who is it you're looking for?

Shed's voice   I'm your neighbor, 'cross the hall.

Pause. **Stephen** *opens.*

Stephen   Hi.

Shed   Hey, 'sup.

Stephen   Not much.

Shed   Yeah. Naw, 'cuz I know you help us out over there.

Stephen Right?

Shed Yeah. You know, I just wanna say, we appreciate that, you helping us out.

Stephen Oh. It's not a problem.

Shed Anything you ever need . . .

Stephen Uh-huh.

Shed You know how it is, we all live together, we all neighbors.

Stephen Uh-huh.

Shed Naw, 'cuz it's good to know, everyone look out for everyone up here . . . everybody let everybody live their lives.

Stephen Right.

Pause

Shed All right. Cool, that's all. Peace.

Shed *extends his hand.* **Stephen** *takes it.* **Shed** *shakes, releases.*

Stephen Bye.

Shed *goes.* **Stephen** *shuts the door.*

Scene Two

Shed's *appartment. He enters.* **Lily** *(who speaks with a British accent tinged with a black American urban sound) is sitting in front of the TV.* **Shed** *sits next to her.*

Lily I heard this funny joke, wanna hear it?

Shed What is it?

Lily Three faggots are milking cows in a/barn

Shed's *cellphone rings. He looks at the number, answers.*

Shed What? No. Not here. I told you. No. Peace.

He hangs up.

Lily   Was that Dave?

Shed   No, it was the boys, looking to party…

Lily   That wasn't Dave?

Shed   I told them, find somewhere else. Keep calling . . .

Lily   – What did you say to the faggot?

Shed   He harmless.

Lily   Is Dave with Maryanne tonight?

Shed   – He fine, just spoke a minute. He not gonna call anybody, he scared.

Lily   Is Dave with Maryanne tonight?

Shed   I don't know, Lily.

Lily   Where is he?

Shed   I don't know.

Lily   What did I do?

Shed   Chill.

Lily   I'm chill.

Shed   – Just a precaution, but – I'm done though. No time for this. What's saved is saved, this is it. There's jobs, you know. Money saved. No need to putting myself through this, stuck here all day, stuck in this place, never going outside, worrying about cops, people in the building knowing what's going on, calling the cops. Done.

Lily   Yeah, but you're used to it. That's the problem. You're used to it, you're used/to –

Shed   Just gotta start. Make this my place, make it peaceful, make the changes, make a home.

Lily   Dave's not gonna be happy. You make him a lot of money. Dave's not gonna/just –

Shed   I understand what Dave think, but he'll find someone else – always someone else.

Lily   Dave likes you. Dave's/not –

Shed   One day you gotta realize you a man.

Lily   You're a boy!

Shed   You realize you a man. One day you stop certain things. Time for certain things to stop. And I'm not gonna fuck you.

Pause.

Lily   You don't know where Dave is?

Shed   Dave's not gonna fuck you either, darling.

Lily   Dave's with Maryanne.

Shed   Dave will fuck Maryanne, Dave not *with* Maryanne. He will fuck you, but he'll never be with you.

Lily   You'll be with me but you won't fuck me.

Shed   No.

Lily   Is it 'cuz we're pals?

Shed   I'm not a boy, I'm a man.

Lily   Men don't fuck?

Shed   That's not what I'm saying.

Lily   Yes you are.

Shed   I'm being a man, there are times you go without things.

Lily   I'm not a thing, a person is not a thing. I'm a person. I'm a/girl.

Shed   Whatever.

Lily   Yeah, you're so funny.

Shed   What I'm saying is, a man conduct his life different, including girls.

Lily   What do you mean?

Shed   Problem with people, they get too ambitious. 'I'm gonna marry this girl.' Unrealistic. 'I'm gonna have a million dollars.' 'I'm gonna get a recording contract.' Why don't you lay down one song first? Why don't you make fifty thousand first, why don't you try fucking the bitch more than two months?

Lily   Me and Dave were together for three months. Maryanne thinks she/can –

Shed   He fucked you for three months, you not together.

Lily   You've only known me one month, what do you know?

Shed   I know when someone is someone and when they not.

Liily   – What's your favorite position for fucking?

Shed   Things happen for real, happen slow.

Lily   You had to pick one, fucking or getting high, which one would you pick?

Shed   Why you ask these questions?

Lily   To see where people stand. If Dave was hurt, would I go to the hospital with flowers? If he was with Maryanne still? Yes. I believe in love.

Timothy *enters from back. He uses crutches with much effort. Pause.*

Timothy   What's on TV?

Shed *doesn't answer.* **Timothy** *goes, off.*

Shed   There's things in life that go on, like where you live, what you have, those things never go away. Getting high goes away, sex goes away, you like having sex with someone then one day you don't. You high at ten o'clock, at two o'clock you not. So if you gotta focus on one thing in life you pick the thing that stays.

This place gonna stay. He's gonna be out, and it's mine.

Lily   Will you still let me come over?

Shed   – Him, no more partying with the boys, and no more dealing. Place gonna be mine.

Lily   Where's he gonna live?

Shed   He had his whole life to figure that out. I watched him, he prepared for nothing.

Lily   But where's he gonna go, you can't/just –

Shed   Where's anybody go? Like, you break with someone, where they go? They figure something out.

Lily (*reaching for her cellphone*)   Do you think Dave's at Maryanne's?

Shed   Why you gonna call him if he there? You know if he be there he not wanting to see you.

Pause.

Lily   I don't know what I/did.

Shed   I'll cuddle you, if you want.

Pause. **Lily** *smiles. They cuddle.*

Lily   Dominic liked to cuddle.

Shed   Who's Dominic?

Lily   My last boyfriend. When he was fucked up, he liked to cuddle.

Shed   What happened to him?

Lily   He went away to see friends and he just stayed. Then I left. I dunno what happened to him. – Do you think Dave and Maryanne are in love?

Timothy *enters from back, eating.*

Timothy   What's on?

Shed (*taking arm away from* **Lily**)   Why you awake?

Timothy   What are you watching?

Shed   Why you be awake all hours, at night you supposed to sleep.

Timothy   I ran out of cigarettes.

Pause. **Shed** *lights a cigarette.* **Timothy** *walks, off.* **Lily** *touches* **Shed***'s crotch.*

Shed   No.

Lily   Why not?

Shed   Nothing happened.

Lily   I don't believe you.

Shed   Ain't nothing happening.

Lily (*continuing to play*)   Not even if I suck it?

Shed   No.

Lily   You're not getting hard!

Shed *puts his arm around her again. She stops touching his crotch. Pause.*

Lily   When I came with Dave that day I thought you were so scary.

Shed   Why?

Lily   You didn't say anything. Would Dave be mad if he knew I was here?

Shed   He's with Maryanne, why he be mad?

Lily   Maryanne thinks she/can –

Shed   You too manic. You gotta learn to settle down. 'Dave, Dave.' Things happen for real when they happen slow.

Shed *kisses her on the head. They watch TV.*

Scene Three

A (relatively) quiet area of the club. **Stephen** *stands next to* **Leo**, *who is Asian. Pause.*

Leo It's so over, isn't it?

Stephen What?

Leo I don't know. All of it.

Stephen Oh.

Leo You didn't look like you were having a good time, so . . .

Stephen I'm just looking for someone.

Leo Who?

Stephen I'm trying to find my boyfriend.

Leo Oh, you lost him?

Stephen I just got here – I can't find him.

Leo Are you on anything?

Stephen Sorry?

Leo Are you on any drugs?

Stephen No.

Leo Drugs are kind of over, too, aren't they? What are we rebelling against except our own feelings?

Stephen Good question.

Pause. **Stephen** *looks around.*

Leo What's he like?

Stephen What does he look like?

Leo That too – but what is he *like*?

Stephen He's sweet, he's sensitive . . .

Leo Do you love him?

Stephen I do. (*Looking.*) There's so many people.

Leo And the lights. And everyone looks alike.

Stephen Uh-huh.

Leo   Or it's just that I look so different. What do you do?

Stephen   I'm a writer.

Leo   Cool – you're smart!

Stephen   I guess.

Leo   I'm in grad school – American studies. Whatever that is. Is your boyfriend white?

Stephen   He is.

Leo   I don't know why I keep coming here – I have no access. I'm totally ignored because I'm not blond and built and – it's like, it's so clear here, like – this is really it, you know. Who cares what we *do* in this world – it's all how you look. Who cares who *speaks* at our funeral. Just go to the gym and sign up. Buy the right clothes.

Stephen   Uh-huh . . .

Leo   – It's like, I look at this and it's like – How can you even believe in homophobia? Gay people are supposed to be oppressed but – come *on*. I mean, I believe in oppression – I believe, like, that Iraqis are oppressed and whole continents are oppressed in brutal ways – but – look at this. – But I guess oppression is tricky, it's more invisible now, more indirect, harder to define. Who do you blame if you can't tell who's oppressing you – you can't have a rally against invisible forces. And why would anyone here want to believe they're oppressed? It's not a pleasant way to live.

Stephen *looks around.* **Leo***'s nose starts to bleed.*

Leo   I guess I'm talking mostly about myself. I guess I just wish I could disappear like everyone else here. I wish I could be as anonymous as them. Or maybe it's the opposite – maybe I just wish someone would look at me. I'd like to have someone who says he loves me looking for me! Maybe I should just join the gym and dye my hair blond.

Stephen *looks at* **Leo.**

Stephen   Oh – are you okay?

Leo   What?

Stephen   Your nose is bleeding, I think.

Leo *touches his lip, feels blood.*

Leo   Oh fuck!

Leo *runs, off.* **Stephen** *sees* **Tyler**, *rushes towards him. The music is deafening.*

Tyler   OH – HEY!

Stephen   HI!

Tyler   YOU'RE HERE!

Stephen   I TRIED CALLING! I GUESS YOU COULDN'T HEAR YOUR PHONE!

Tyler   WHAT?

Stephen   NOTHING. YOU LOOK GREAT!

Tyler   THANK YOU. YOU TOO. SO THE PLAN CHANGED A LITTLE.

Stephen   WHAT?

Tyler   THE PLAN CHANGED A LITTLE. I WASN'T GOING TO – BUT I ENDED UP TAKING ECSTASY.

Stephen   Oh.

Tyler   IT'S ACTUALLY BEEN TERRIBLE – NOT THE ECSTASY BUT – IT TURNS OUT BILLY'S FRIEND MICHAEL IS HERE? AND RUSSELL AND KEITH AND DEREK ARE HERE TOO, YOU DON'T KNOW THEM BUT – IT'S TURNED INTO THIS WHOLE – LET ME FIND BILLY AND TELL HIM I'M LEAVING. IS THAT OKAY?

Stephen   WHY ARE YOU HAVING A TERRIBLE TIME?

Tyler   LET ME FIND BILLY.

Stephen   OKAY.

Tyler   I'LL TELL BILLY I'M LEAVING.

Tyler *goes, off. A* **Young White Man** *comes to* **Stephen** *and begins dancing, somewhat seductively, but with a ridiculous seriousness.* **Stephen** *dances with him, politely, avoiding eye contact.* **Young White Man** *demands to be seen, keeps dancing into* **Stephen**'s *vision.* **Stephen** *smiles and dances away from him.* **Young White Man** *follows him.* **Stephen** *goes back to the quiet area of the club.* **Young White Man** *dances away.* **Leo** *returns, holding a napkin to his nose, pinching, checking.*

Leo   Thanks for telling me.

Stephen   Oh – yeah –

Leo   What do you write about? One of my areas of study is queer representation.

Stephen   I actually can't really talk, I found my boyfriend, so –

Leo   Oh, you found him?

Stephen (*sees* **Tyler**, *turns briefly back to* **Leo**) – Nice to meet you.

Leo   You're going?

Stephen *goes back into the loud part of the club.*

Tyler   HEY – WHERE DID YOU GO?

Stephen   WHAT?

Tyler   WERE YOU TALKING TO SOMEONE?

Stephen   NO.

Tyler   WHO WAS THAT?

Stephen   NO ONE.

Tyler   SO – UM. THERE'S A PROBLEM.

Stephen   WHAT?

Tyler   WHAT?

Stephen   WHAT'S THE PROBLEM?

Tyler   WELL – WE JUST STARTED PEAKING? SO BILLY'S LIKE, WHY AM I LEAVING NOW, WHEN WE JUST STARTED PEAKING.

Stephen   DO YOU WANT TO TALK IN A QUIETER PART?

Tyler   WHAT?

Stephen   COME TO THE QUIETER PART!

Tyler   OKAY.

They go to the quieter part of the club. **Leo** *sits some feet away, watching.*

Stephen   What's going on?

Tyler   It's kind of a long story.

Stephen   You said you're having a terrible time?

Tyler   Well, it's this whole thing. Michael's here, and you met Michael, and his boyfriend Russell, and there are these two guys, Keith and Derek, who you don't know, I don't think.

Stephen   Uh-huh?

Tyler   Anyway, so we were all dancing, me and Billy and all six of us basically, and, Billy's had a crush on Keith for a while. So basically Michael and Russell start dancing in their own world, so it's me and Billy and Keith and Derek. So I'm dancing with Derek because it's clear Billy wants to dance with Keith. Then Derek starts dancing with some random guy, and he disappears. So it's me and Billy and Keith, and I don't, I don't mind dancing in my own world, so I just drift away a little so Billy can dance with Keith. Also we did some coke. Anyway. So I'm dancing in my own world, but Keith keeps dancing towards me – but not just dancing towards me, he's doing this move, this really, like, provocative move, this kind of 'dance walk'?

Stephen   Uh-huh . . .

Tyler   Sort of . . . he'll dance-walk towards Billy, but at the last moment, at the moment he gets to Billy, it's kind of a diva move, just as he reaches Billy he turns away and dances back towards me. So he's going between me and Billy, but he's dancing more with me – he just, it's sort of like he's teasing Billy. And Billy says to him, he grabs him and says, 'Why won't you dance with me?' and Keith's like, 'What are you talking about?' So Billy tells him to fuck off. Just says fuck off. And Keith's playing all naïve and Billy's just tearing into him, and Keith just up and walks away. And I say, 'I guess it's just me and you,' and he gets really mad and he says, 'No, it's you and *Stephen* and *fuck* you too.' And then I saw you.

Billy *enters.*

Billy   Hey.

Tyler *stands, moves to* **Billy**; **Stephen** *hangs back.* **Leo** *looks at him.*

Tyler   Hey.

Billy   I can't believe you're going.

Tyler   I don't –

Billy   You don't make a plan for an evening and then bail out.

Tyler   Billy, you told me to –

Billy   Just stay, we made a plan. Come on.

Tyler   I just . . . Stephen doesn't want to stay, he doesn't really like clubs . . .

Young White Man *enters, sits next to* **Leo**. **Leo** *hides his napkin.*

Leo   Hi!

Young White Man *nods.*

Billy   Fine. Go play boyfriend.

Tyler   *Billy* . . .

Billy   And this fucking E I got sucks.

Pause.

Tyler   Bye.

Tyler *goes back to* **Stephen**. **Billy** *stays where he is.* **Stephen** *rises, and* **Tyler** *and* **Stephen** *go, off.* **Billy** *looks briefly at* **Leo**, *then makes sustained eye contact with* **Young White Man**. **Billy** *goes, off.* **Young White Man** *follows him, off.* **Leo** *watches, then looks around.*

Scene Four

Stephen *and* **Tyler** *enter* **Stephen**'s *apartment.* **Tyler** *sits down, sees an open book, picks it up and reads.*

Tyler   'In the end, a whole vast area of Central Africa was completely transformed, not by the actions of some power or international organization.'

Stephen   It's such a good little book, this British historian Eric Hobsbawm . . .

Tyler *reads with a British accent.*

Tyler   'Everyone got involved: Paris, Washington, and the United Nations. Everyone tried to mediate and, I am told, there were as many as thirteen different mediators in Rwanda. However, it all proved to be inadequate.'

He puts down the book.

Did I tell you about this audition tomorrow?

Stephen   No. What's it for?

Tyler   This TV show? Want a massage?

Stephen   Sure!

Tyler *massages* **Stephen**.

Tyler   It's not terrible. It's about this kind of loser kid in a small town who learns he has special powers.

Stephen (*derisively*)   Special powers?

Tyler   I love you.

Stephen *picks up book.*

Stephen   Listen to this.

Tyler   I said I love you!

Stephen   I love you too! 'A Marxist interpretation suggests that, in having understood a particular historical stage is not permanent, human society is a successful structure because it is capable of change, and thus the present is not its point of arrival.'

Tyler (*mockingly*)   Marxist!

Stephen (*laughs*)   Interpretation, though. There's a difference.

Tyler   That *is* beautiful. You're tense.

Stephen   I am?

Tyler   Supertense.

Stephen   I guess I got a little freaked out tonight.

Tyler   What happened?

Stephen   It's not a big deal really.

Tyler   Am I hurting you?

Stephen (*laughing*)   I can't tell, I think you might be. Yeah, the kid from across the hall knocked on my door.

Tyler   Why?

Stephen   Well, this other kid – this white kid – who I assume was here to buy drugs, but he went to the wrong apartment – knocked on my door. Anyway – he must have told this to the kid across the hall, and the kid – the black kid – must know I help out his dad or whatever, so he must think that maybe I know what's going on in there, and he just sort of wanted to let me know that he knew I knew what was going on – that he's dealing.

Pause

Tyler   Did he threaten you?

Stephen   No, no. I'm sure he's harmless, but . . .

Tyler   Be careful, Stephen.

Stephen   No, I know.

Tyler   Okay, now me.

Stephen *massages* **Tyler**.

Tyler   I got a little freaked out tonight, too.

Stephen   Yeah

Tyler   I was talking to some people at the club. I talked to this kid who said he was nineteen? He said he was a pig bottom and was looking for someone to fuck him.

Stephen   Uh-huh.

Tyler   And then I met this woman who said she was a slave and introduced me to her master.

Stephen   Right.

Tyler   Oooh, right there. Yeah. I don't know, it started to depress me.

Stephen   Yeah. Well, to be around people who are degrading themselves is depressing.

Tyler   I don't know why it depressed me so much, though. It shouldn't.

Stephen   Well . . . that sounds like a very sensitive response.

Tyler   The pig-bottom kid was so young.

Stephen   Uh-huh.

Tyler   How did he get like that? But I don't know why it upset me so much.

Stephen   Well – maybe you identify with it.

Tyler   What do you mean?

Stephen   Well – we grew up with homophobia, in our families, in school – so we know what it's like to have our sexuality and a degraded sense of self linked.

Tyler   Right. That's where we come from.

Stephen   Maybe it doesn't go away – even here.

Tyler   I just read that HIV rates for people our age are going up, did you see that?

Stephen   God, that's unfathomable to me – that people are having unsafe/sex.

Tyler*'s cellphone rings. He checks it.*

Tyler   It's Billy. I'm not gonna answer it.

Stephen (*laughing*)   Billy calling to tell you to fuck off again?

Tyler   He probably met some guy and wants to tell me all about it and ask me if he should go home with him. 'He's cute but he's not *hot*, I don't know, he has a nice *ass* . . .'

Stephen   Ha. But really. I think – if it depresses you – being in those situations, with people like that – you should pay attention to that.

Tyler   But it shouldn't depress me. It's the way things are, you should be able to look at the way things/are.

His cellphone rings again. He answers.

Hello? Okay. Thank you. Okay. I have to go. I love you too.

He hangs up.

Billy apologizes. He wanted to tell me he loves me.

Stephen   Uh-huh . . . so . . . Billy really hates me, doesn't he?

Tyler   No – why do you say that?

Stephen   He's never very polite to me. He didn't even look at me at the/club.

Tyler   Part of that was the ecstasy – we got our pills from different guys, I got mine from this guy Derek knew, but that guy didn't have that many, so Billy had to just sort of find his own and I don't think his were that good.

Stephen   He got the 'fuck off' ecstasy.

Tyler   Billy's Billy. I've known him for so long, I guess I'm just used to him. He didn't have the easiest life, so he's sort of abrasive. You either get his world or you don't, is how he looks at it.

Pause.

Stephen   'Billy's Billy.'

Tyler   What?

Stephen   I don't know . . . I mean, someone says 'Fuck off' to you . . .

Tyler   It's hard for Billy – he doesn't have a boyfriend, his career isn't going well, sometimes people don't take him seriously because he's so campy . . .

Stephen   Well, you have to take yourself seriously.

Tyler   Like you, you silly goose! Mr Serious!

Stephen   Ha.

A knock on the door. Pause.

What time is it?

He gets up, goes to the door. **Tyler** *rises.*

Hello?

Timothy's voice   Hey, I heard you were up, I'm sorry, do you have two cigarettes you could lend me?

Tyler (*muted*)   Tell him you quit.

Pause. **Stephen** *opens the door.*

Timothy   Hi.

Stephen   Hey.

He gives him three cigarettes.

Here you go.

Timothy   Hey, you know, my check is late, you know? It was supposed to/come –

Stephen   Uh-huh?

Timothy   And I have to go to the hospital tomorrow, and the Medicaid is all – and my check is late – I'm trying to get, I'm trying to get this leg, keeps being delayed – if you got ten dollars, I pay you back when my check comes. Two days late now, nothing I can do . . .

Stephen   Sure.

Stephen *gives him ten dollars.*

Timothy   God bless you.

Timothy *goes.* **Stephen** *locks the door. Pause.*

Tyler   Ten dollars?

Stephen   – What?

Tyler   I just – that makes me worried.

Stephen   Worried about what?

Tyler   Just – that he'll think – you're a pushover.

Stephen   Right. But – his check hasn't come.

Tyler   You believe that?

Stephen   Yeah – I think it's pretty common, actually. Social security, disability – I think the checks only come once a month. It's a disaster for people when they don't come on time.

Tyler   But if his son is dealing drugs . . . and *threatened* you tonight . . .

Stephen   He didn't *threaten*/me.

Tyler   Like, what if they're working as a team or something? Like, now they know you're scared, so they can ask you for money and you'll be scared so you give it to them.

Stephen   I don't – think he and his son get along. His son won't buy him cigarettes . . . I mean, if he comes tomorrow and asks for ten more dollars, I won't give it to him, but . . .

Tyler   But what if they're, like, working as a team?

Pause.

I don't know. I just worry. I get scared for you. I love you and – a cigarette, okay. But ten dollars – you can't help everyone, people have to take care of themselves.

Stephen   Well, you – you know, I mean – like – your trust fund helps you, right.

Tyler   What do you mean?

Stephen   You don't have to worry the way most people do.

Tyler   But I *do* stuff. My acting class, going to the gym, preparing for auditions.

Stephen   I'm just saying – you know, he doesn't have any protection. He's black, he's –

Tyler   But what I'm saying is, what if he just takes that money and buys alcohol? You don't know/what he –

Stephen   I drink, we all – everyone drinks – you're on drugs now. I mean – you just said. Talking to these people in the club – made you sad. He – makes me sad. That he's in trouble the way he is, that makes me sad. So – I feel better helping him.

Tyler   Yeah, but I was in a club, I didn't – try to help anyone. I'm never going to see those people again.

Stephen   Exactly. I – he's right across the hall. I see him every day. He needs help . . .

Tyler   But you don't *know*.

Stephen   Know what?

Tyler   You have no idea what his life is really like, and I don't see how you/think you –

Stephen   There *are* facts.

Tyler   You don't know –

Stephen   – He has no leg.

Pause.

Tyler   I'm sorry. I just – I had a bad night. And I don't – want you to get taken advantage of. People with good hearts, they get hurt in this world. They do . . .

Stephen   I understand your concern . . . but – I think I'm okay here . . .

Pause. **Tyler** *moves to* **Stephen**, *kisses him. They kiss rather madly, and undress each other.*

Stephen   I love you.

Tyler   I love you so much, Stephen.

Stephen   Oh, Tyler . . .

Scene Five

Timothy *struggles into his apartment, carrying a large brown paper bag in his mouth.* **Lily** *watches TV.* **Shed** *is asleep on the couch.* **Timothy** *shuts door, leans against wall, takes bag with hand, goes over to chair, sits.*

Timothy   He sleeping?

Lily   Yeah

Timothy *takes a forty ounce of beer out of the bag, along with a pack of Newports and a candy bar.*

Timothy   Can I ask you, are you with Shed?

Lily   No. I was with Dave.

Timothy   Dave. You here, though, a lot.

Lily   Me and Shed are pals.

Timothy   Oh.

Lily   We're buddies! We're buds!

Timothy   I don't know about Shed. He don't have girls around a lot anymore.

Lily   He's a big boy now.

Timothy   Yeah?

They laugh. **Timothy** *lights a cigarette, laughs.*

Where are the boys?

Lily   He doesn't want the boys here anymore.

Timothy   Why not?

Lily   He's a big boy, I'm telling you. No boys, no girls, no drugs.

Timothy   No – weed?

Lily   No – weed. But no drugs.

Timothy   Huh. So you with Dave.

Lily   Can I have a cigarette?

Timothy   You don't got any?

Lily   Smoked them all.

Timothy *gives her a cigarette.*

Timothy   I used to drive trucks. Now I can't drive. I had a good/career.

Lily   I got here, I met Dave, we fell in love. We were together three months.

Timonthy   Three months . . .

Lily   You have sex?

Timothy   Sex? What are you? Ha! I got a photo album of me from before – I could show you pictures of/me –

Lily   You don't have sex anymore?

Timothy *drinks.*

Timothy   I don't know, that might be over, all that. Nobody wants to sleep with someone who has no leg.

Lily   Awww. Maybe there's a woman with no leg, too.

Timothy   I never seen a woman with one leg. Well, that's not true. But I wouldn't want a woman with one leg!

Pause.

Two things make people sleep with you is, you have a job or you're young. I'm old with no job. If you look at pictures of me, I was/living a good –

Lily   Do you jerk off at least?

Pause. **Timothy** *drinks.*

Timothy   I used to be a janitor before I was a truck driver. I can't do that either. Where are you from?

Lily   England. Fucking dreary. The weather sucks, everything is old – no one's happy there, nothing's fresh. America has a different energy, do you know what I mean?

Timothy   Is he trying to get me out of here?

Pause.

Lily   I dunno. That's sad.

Timothy   What?

Lily   That no one wants to sleep with you.

Timothy   Oh.

Lily   Does your dick work?

Timothy   Wh? – Yeah – it works, it wasn't damaged.

Lily   When's the last time a lady touched it?

Timothy   My wife.

Lily *goes over to* **Timothy** *and touches his crotch.*

Timothy   What are you? . . .

She unzips him, puts her hand inside, fondles him for some time.

Stop.

Lily   It's okay, you're getting hard.

Timothy   No.

Lily   There. That's nice. Is that nice?

Timothy   Y – yeah.

Lily (*still masturbating him*)   Yeah . . . that's nice . . . Does Shed have any other girls over?

Timothy   I haven't seen any. . .

Lily   Really? No?

Timothy *shakes his head no.* **Lily** *continues to masturbate him. Then her cell phone rings. She stops, looks at the number, answers it.*

Liily   Hello? Hi, Dave. Nowhere, just hanging. Nothing. Where you at?

Pause.

Fuck her, she's a stupid cunt anyway. Okay!

She hangs up and gathers her things.

Timothy   You're going?

Lily *goes back to* **Timothy**, *puts her hand in his pants again.*

Lily   I bet you could come really fast for me.

She masturbates him for a while. He orgasms, stifling sound. She takes her hand out of his pants, wipes it on his pants, giggles.

I gotta go. See you later, big sexy man!

Timothy   Bye . . .

Lily *goes off. Door slams.* **Shed** *stirs a little.* **Timothy** *starts to cry. He zips up his pants, tucks in his shirt.* **Shed** *awakens.* **Timothy** *stops crying. He quickly lights a cigarette.* **Shed** *looks at* **Timothy**.

Shed   . . . You stealin' from me when I sleep?

Timothy   No, these aren't Camels. These are Newports. These are mine.

Shed   The faggot give 'em to you?

Timothy   I bought them.

Shed   Why you crying?

Timothy   I'm not. I was just thinking.

Shed   Where's Lily?

Timothy   She left.

Shed   She left? What, you scare her off?

Timothy   No.

Shed   When you gettin' your leg? Sick of this shit already.

Timothy   They keep saying next week! Next week. Then they say, there's some/reason –

Shed   – Talking her ear off. You annoy people, you talk too much, you don't/do anything –

Timothy   No, Dave called. She went to Dave.

Pause. **Shed** *looks for a cigarette, his pack is empty.*

You all out? Want one?

Shed *keeps looking in empty packs, lifting things. He gets angry.*

Timothy   You want one? Here

Shed *goes over to* **Timothy**, *takes his pack away from him. He goes to the couch. He lights a cigarette. He looks at* **Timothy**.

Timothy   Come on. Gimme back.

Shed *goes to the stereo, puts in a CD.*

Shed. Gimme one, just to wake up to. One to go to sleep and one to/wake up to.

Over the stereo an Eminem-like rapper blasts. **Shed** *sits down on the couch.*

Eminem-like rapper

> Don't give me no fag on the corner in the park
> walking like a girl looking like a shark
> trying to get at my balls
> bitch get ready to fall
> make a pass?
> fag, I'll take that ass
> and put it in a cast.
> Shit, what time is it?
> eleven o'clock
> here, suck on this
> no not my cock
> boy, this a Glock

Timothy *rises. He goes, off, with his forty and his candy bar.* **Shed** *moves to the song.*

Eminem-like rapper

> 'cuz I don't take that
> naw I don't take that
> boy I ain't take that
> shit, who gon' take that

Lights rise on **Stephen** *and* **Tyler**. *They are making out, naked. They can clearly hear the song.* **Stephen** *stops.*

Tyler   What?

Stephen   This song.

Tyler   I know – Don't worry about it.

The song continues. **Tyler** *kisses* **Stephen**, *they continue to make out.*

Eminem-like rapper

> Shit, you gon' fake that?
> naw, don't you take that.

Shed *rises, starts acting out the song, as if performing it.*

Eminem-like rapper

> Damn, when I was six
> Growin' up in the proj-ix
> with my bitch mom
> every night she was gone
> so my Uncle Rick'd babysit
> and try to get in my shit
> 'Wanna play hide and seek?'
> Uncle Rick, Uncle Rick
> why you peek
> at my little dick?
> That shit's sick
> so suck
> suck
> no not on me
> man, suck this blade
> swallow your tongue
> watch your faggot life fade
> next I'm'a puncture your lung

Stephen *pulls away from* **Tyler**.

Stephen   I can't.

Tyler   Just block it out. I'm here. Think about me.

Stephen   I – I/just –

Tyler *leans in, kisses* **Stephen**. *He fellates* **Stephen**.

Eminem-like rapper

> 'cuz I don't take that
> naw I don't take that

Song continues. **Stephen** *orgasms.*

Stephen   Ohh!–

Scene Six

Slide reads: August 2, 2001

Stephen *and* **Patricia** *in a museum. In one corner, a black* **Security Guard** *crosses on and off. In another, a* **Violinist** *plays.* **Stephen** *and* **Patricia** *speak quietly, moving slowly across the stage. A* **Young Art Student**, *sloppily dressed, sketches, looking in* **Patricia**'s *direction. He wears headphones and moves somewhat to their music.*

Patricia   It's good you're having a party. That's beautiful.

Stephen   It'll be a little hot, but I guess that's okay.

Patricia   Frank's gonna come, which is a miracle. – Isn't that beautiful?

Stephen   It's so chaotic. All that color.

Patricia   I don't understand this violinist – since when does art need music to go along/with it?

Stephen   I read about this, museum attendance is down, they did focus groups, people think museums are dull, so they're trying new things to attract more visitors.

Patricia   Great, next it'll be strippers holding up the paintings.

Stephen   Do you think people – do you think – how do you think people change?

Patricia   What's this about?

Stephen   Just a question.

Patricia   It's about Tyler.

Stephen   Well – yeah, but – generally, I mean . . .

Patricia   But there's a specific . . .?

Stephen   We just – the other night –

Patricia   Is that kid drawing us?

Stephen   What?

Patricia   That kid behind us.

Stephen *looks briefly at* **Young Art Student,** *who stops sketching when he does, then resumes sketching when* **Stephen** *turns away.*

Stephen   I think he is. – Yeah, it was just – Tyler and I got into it about my neighbor again the other night, he was upset that I gave him ten dollars.

Patricia   We should probably keep our voices down a little.

Stephen   Oh – yeah, I'm sorry.

Patricia (*moving to next painting*)   Mm-hmm? – What year is this?

Stephen   – I just, I wondered what I could have said to him to make him *see* more . . .

Patricia   Well – you know, you have to be gentle because – and patient. Think of where Tyler's coming from. You know, you dealt with your trauma by identifying with the pain of others, trying to understand it, in order to solve it. So maybe you're empathetic, but his history hasn't allowed him to develop – (*Looks back at* **Young Art Student**.) He is, he's drawing us.

Stephen (*derisively*)   I think I saw a Ralph Nader sticker on his bookbag.

Patricia   How rude is that. Who goes to a museum to draw people? Look at the paintings.

Stephen   Maybe you're inspiring him.

Patricia   Great, I'm glad I can be of service.

Patricia *moves to next painting.* **Violinist** *begins new song.* **Stephen** *follows, looking briefly at* **Young Art Student**.

Stephen   – But maybe I *should* have better tried to explain to Tyler why he thinks the way he does.

Patricia   Well – people have a lot to think about on their own without thinking about how they think.

Stephen   What do you mean?

Patricia   Maybe you have to learn to tolerate a certain amount of narcissism, you know? It's not easy to be alive and – all this, all these right and wrong ways to think – I think you should make room for just – who people are. Without feeling you need/to change –

Stephen   But that's really scary, to think that way, it's so/defeated.

Patricia   – I need to sit, I have a headache.

Stephen   Art gives you headaches.

Patricia   It's not – talking and looking at paintings, it's a little/much.

Stephen   I'm sorry, I know I'm/babbling.

Patricia   No, it's – you're asking valid questions, it's just . . .

They go to a bench. **Young Art Student** *gets up, moves behind them, continues sketching.*

I don't know. When I listen to you, I hear this – you're always looking for something that isn't there – something better – as opposed to reality. Who someone might be instead of who they are.

Stephen   Uh-huh? . . .

Patricia   I think you're setting yourself up when you look at things like that. – Okay, this has to stop.

Stephen   What?

Patricia *turns to* **Young Art Student** *and stares at him directly.* **Stephen** *follows.* **Young Art Student** *goes, off. The* **Security Guard** *laughs, crosses off as well.*

Patricia   How rude is that? Visual artists, my God. Voyeurs.

Stephen   Maybe he'll go home and create a masterpiece.

Pause. The **Violinist** *begins a new song.*

I don't know. When I look at him – I just – I can feel it. I can feel what it was like to *be* him. You know Tyler tried to kill himself? Almost every gay man I know my age either tried to kill himself or fantasized about it.

Patricia   He tried to kill himself?

Stephen   Well, not exactly – he drove his father's truck to a cliff, and he sat there, the engine idling, trying to get up the courage to drive over. When he was sixteen. And I put myself there. I'm beside him. I'm with him at the edge of the cliff, passenger side.

Patricia   Empathy.

Stephen   Love.

Patricia   Mm. What's the difference, I wonder.

Pause.

Stephen   I hope people have fun at my party.

Patricia   I hope *you* have fun at your party.

They laugh.

Act Two

Scene One

Slide reads: August 2, 2001.

Timothy*'s apartment.* **Shed** *and* **Lily** *cuddle on the couch.* **Lily***'s eye is very badly bruised, swollen black.*

The TV is on. **Timothy** *enters. He sits down on the couch next to* **Shed** *and* **Lily***.*

Timothy   What's this?

Neither answers.

Ha! Oh, this show is a funny one.

Neither says anything. **Timothy** *looks over briefly at* **Lily,** *who does not return the look. He gets up and goes, off.* **Shed***'s cellphone rings. He picks it up, looks at it.*

Shed   Dave.

Lily   Dave?

Shed *answers the phone.*

Shed   Hello? Yeah. Come up.

He hangs up.

Lily   Where is he?

Shed   He outside.

Lily   What should I do, stay here or go?

Shed   Up to you.

Lily   I'm scared.

Shed   No reason to be scared.

Lily   He won't go in back, will he?

Shed   No. he not gonna care – he gonna be like, 'Okay, you don't wanna deal, okay,' 'cuz I'm just gonna say it simple, and he gonna go.

Lily   He won't go in back?

Shed   No need to get so crazy, now.

Lily   I'm scared though! What if he sees me! What if he hits me again!

Shed   Why he be mad at you? It happened, isolated, you didn't do nothing to him, he probably forgot.

Lily   – He was really angry at Maryanne, he took it out on me.

Shed   Stop – you getting all confused now. Just relax.

Lily   What if he tells you? What if he tells you you/can't stop?

Shed   Why he want trouble? Go in the back, nothing gonna happen, if for some reason it does, I'm gonna be okay.

Lily   Be careful. He loses his temper and gets crazy –

Shed   He gonna be up here, so go back.

Lily   Okay.

He kisses her on the head. She gets up and goes in back, off. **Shed** *takes brass knuckles out and puts them in his pocket. An insistent, manic knock on the door.* **Shed** *answers it.* **Dave** *enters. He speaks in an affected manner, often using black rhythm and emphasis without mimicking black pronunciation – his accent is that of a white upper-class person.*

Dave   What's up, dog!

Shed   What's up.

Dave *looks around.* **Shed** *shuts the door.*

Dave   Looking nice in here, looking neat. Where your boys at?

Shed   I told them, find some other place to party. Too crazy 'round here.

Dave   Lily said, Lily said. What's up, man!

Shed   Not much, not much, you.

Dave   Other than the bitches, everything is sweet, – I'm *rolling* right now.

Shed   Yeah?

Dave   Three pills. *Good* ecstasy, very clean, I met this guy, European motherfucker, shit's hot!

He flips through channels on TV.

Yeah, man, my mom wanted to have a *talk* tonight. Where can I go, like – the rehab talk. I couldn't deal, so I took three pills. Told her I had a headache, told her they were aspirin! She believed me!

Shed (*laughs*)   Aw.

Dave   She's like, 'You're twenty.' She's like, 'I remember you. You were a *sweet* boy. You were *sensitive*. What *happened*?' Truth, though – I was fucked *up*, dog! I was never *sweet*. One thing I did, I never told anyone this, I forgot about it, until she was talking – I started rolling, and remembered – I remembered I used to be able, I could hear my parents *fucking*, and I was four*teen* maybe, and I would go the bedroom *door*, and I would – when they were fucking, I would jack *off* – I would hear them – I would hear my stepfather slap my mother's ass – or else it was her slapping *his* ass – and I would jack off picturing it and listening to it!

Shed   Damn.

Dave   'Sensitive.' I would *come* on the *carpet* and I would rub it into the carpet with my *foot*.'

Shed   Damn, why you do that?

Dave   She's like, 'You were a good child.' She's like, 'Why are all your friends *black*?'

Shed   How she know that?

Dave   Fuck, I have people over how. You gotta come over and see this shit.

He sniffs cocaine.

'You've changed.' But nothing changed – that's what I'm realizing, sitting there rolling.

Shed   What you mean?

Dave   I was *always* like this, I just didn't know what to *do*. Like, why you do jack off when you hear your parents fucking? – I tried to fuck the au *pair* when I was fifteen!

Shed   What's that?

Dave   The *maid* – the black *maid*, I tried to *fuck* her.

Shed   Oh.

Dave   I didn't know what I was doing but. It was funny, I tried to *hug* her. I didn't know how to do it so I *hugged* her. Bitch hugged me back! I think I came right then!

Shed   Damn.

Dave   What I'm saying is, I realized I always liked black people – always – and my mother's like, 'You changed.' But I'm thinking how *wrong* she is – I was always fucked up, I just acted different when I got older. But I never changed – I still jack off!

Shed   Yeah.

Dave   I think fucking is like jacking off except there's a pussy instead of your hand! Shit's the same!

He laughs. He hits a music video channel; we hear the Eminem-like song from earlier; it plays quietly throughout the scene.

He's so over, don't you think?

Shed   Oh yeah – he done.

Dave   – Old Timmy here? Old man beating off back there?

Shed   He here, he here.

Dave   He's eating pepperoni?

Shed   I don't know.

Dave   Every time I see him, he's eating, I think, like, what, is he trying to grow a new leg? A new leg made of fat, like, if he keeps eating he'll grow a new leg made of fat?

Shed   Shit's fucked up, Medicaid, I don't know, keeps getting delayed, his new leg. He supposed to be getting it – on my fucking tit all the time, you know?

Dave   Things don't change, I'm telling you. Nothing changes, man. Nothing changes!

Shed   Yeah.

Dave   Who are you sleeping with now?

Shed   Me? I don't know.

Dave   I'm manic, man, I apologize. Bump?

Shed   Naw, I'm okay.

Dave   I'm fucking manic. Have a bump.

Pause. **Shed** *does a bump of cocaine.*

Lily thinks you're gay, dog.

Shed   What?

Dave   She tells me you're gay!

Shed   What!

Dave   How long is it since we met, a year?

Shed   Yeah – since I met you in the club? A year. Lily said/that?

Dave   Dude, I was fucking her in the ass – Lily? – 'cuz she likes that, goddam, British girls, right? – but I was fucking her in the ass and the bitch wasn't clean! I was like, You want people to fuck you in the ass, you best be clean, doll!

Shed   Damn.

Dave   Shit, but I like it dirty anyway, it's all good. Then I was fucking her straight and I was, like, Can I smack you a little? She was like, Yeah, and then she was like, You can smack me harder! So I started smacking her, she's grooving on that, she's saying it's turning her on more, so she's like, she tells me to punch her when I come. I was like, Punch you? She was like, Yeah! She said it was the best she came in a long time.

Shed   Damn.

Dave   Don't worry about what she says, that girl is *crazy*, – You have the cash?

Shed   – Yeah.

Shed *reaches into his pocket, takes out a wad of bills. Dave takes a long knife out of his backpack.*

Dave   Look at this, beautiful, right?

Shed   Wow.

Dave   I decided to start collecting knives.

He hands **Shed** *the knife.*

Dave   Antique, ivory handle, fucking gorgeous, right?

Shed   Wow.

Pause. **Dave** *takes the knife back from* **Shed**, *puts the knife in his bag.* **Shed** *holds out the cash to him.*

Dave   You know what? I had a good day.

He nods for **Shed** *to keep the money, rises.*

My mom went to the Hamptons, I'm gonna go home and party in her bed now.

Shed (*still holding out money*)   No, man, take/it.

Dave   Keep it, dog.

He takes package of cocaine from the bag, gives it to **Shed**, *who now has money in one hand, cocaine in the other.* **Dave** *slings his backpack over his shoulder.*

Lily said it got quiet here. It's quiet here!

Shed *rises.*

Shed   Yeah, I got some stuff coming up, I got to ask you about something.

Dave   I'm fucking manic today, I apologize. – Damn, you got that hungry look in your eyes.

Shed   I do?

Dave   We need to find you some pussy, I think.

Shed   Ha, no, I'm all right.

Dave   Let's get you some pussy. When's the last time you fucked the shit out of a girl, for real?

Shed   I'm okay, take care of myself.

Dave   Dude – come to my house with me.

Shed   That's all right. But if we could/talk.

Dave   Timmy can take care of himself for a night! (*Yelling*). Right, Timmy?

Shed   No, I should/stay.

Dave   You know I love you?

Pause. He wipes a tear from his eye. **Shed** *laughs it off.*

No – I don't just say that 'cuz I'm rolling. But, like, that we can be friends, from such different worlds. That's amazing. That didn't used to be the way it was. But it's that way now. People from different groups. People from different worlds. That's so beautiful – you know how special that is?

Shed   Yeah – I just. I – I never meant to get so deep in dealing.

Pause.

Dave   Oh. You want to *talk*. You're, like – taking stock of your/life.

Shed   Yeah, if we could/talk.

Dave   Bottle of wine, blow, talk all night – if you want to roll, call my European boy – we can sit out on the terrace. You can see the whole city, look out, king of the world, for real!

Shed   I'd like to, but I/have to–

Dave   Let's call some girls and start putting an/itinerary together.

Dave *dials on his cellphone.*

Shed   No, I really can't,/man.

Dave   Show Lily who's a/faggot.

Shed   I would/but –

We hear a cellphone ring loudly. Short pause.

Dave   Shit, did I call you by mistake?

Shed *looks at the ringing cellphone.* **Dave** *looks at his.*

Dave   No, I called Lily.

Shed   – She's – she left her –

Dave   – Is she here?–

Shed   She – she's/napping or something.

Lily *enters.*

Lily   Hi, Dave.

Dave   What are you doing here?

Shed   No, yeah – Lily just hangin'–

Dave *looks at* **Shed**. *Pause.* **Shed** *braces himself. Then* **Dave** *laughs.*

Dave   Whatever. Lily we're going up to my mom's, you gotta come.

Shed   Okay!

Dave   Who else can I call? Or should it just be us three?

Shed   I don't/think –

Dave   Where's Maryanne?

Shed   I don't know and I don't *wanna* know.

Lily   You're rolling.

Dave   How'd you know?

Lily   You're so nice when you're rolling. You're face looks so sweet.

Dave   Let's go.

Lily   Okay.

Lily *takes her cellphone.* **Shed** *doesn't move.*

Shed   I g-g-gotta – I gotta – hang out, I can't – maybe later, when he goes to sleep, but . . .

Pause.

Dave   Okay, call me later. Peace, brother.

Shed   Yeah, peace.

Lily   Bye!

Lily *and* **Dave** *go, off.* **Shed** *stands, still holding the coke and the cash.*

Scene Two

Stephen's *bedroom. Party in progress outside the bedroom; each time the door opens, loud music and party sounds increase.* **Billy** *and* **Patricia** *are talking, both with a drink in their hand.*

Billy   But I have to admit, the rhymes are great, the music is really interesting – he's really hot – I don't agree with what he's saying, but he definitely represents what's already out there, he didn't cause it.

Patricia   Yeah. That's an interesting point.

Pause. Off, music is changed.

So how long have you been friends with Tyler?

Billy   Since college. Okay, can I confide in you? Can I make you my little confidante?

Patricia   What – what do you want to/tell me?

Billy   – Oh God, this – who is putting this awful solemn *music* on?

Patricia   It's probably Frank, my boyfriend – he doesn't like parties, this is what he does, he fiddles with music. It's like he wants to make everyone as miserable as he is.

Billy   Well, *we* have the majority here. It's not 1993 and we are *not* in Seattle!

Patricia   I'll tell him to change it.

Billy   I want to *dance*. Do you dance, Patricia?

Patricia   I do.

Billy   Okay, go yell at your boyfriend and come back and I'll tell you my secret.

Patricia *laughs and goes, off.* **Stephen** *enters*

Stephen   Oh. Was Patricia in here?

Billy   She just went out to change the music. Can I ask you a question?

Stephen   Sure.

Billy   Is there any cocaine here?

Stephen   Um – I haven't seen any.

Billy (*faux sheepishly*)   Do you hate cocaine?

Stephen   Um – I don't make a point of it but – occasionally I do/like it.

Billy   I think this party could use some cocaine.

Stephen Um. Let me look around.

Stephen *exits, off. Music, off, goes from rock to dance mix.*

Billy Yes!

He starts to dance. **Tyler** *enters, dancing.*

There you are!

Tyler Hi!

Patricia *enters.*

Billy Patricia, I love this song!

Patricia My boyfriend hates me now.

Billy *starts dancing with* **Patricia**. *The three dance.* **Stephen** *enters.*

Billy Anything?

Stephen What's Adderall? There are boys in there who say they have Adderall.

Patricia Adderall? My eight-year-old niece is/on Adderall.

Billy It's a prescription drug for attention-deficit disorder, it's of the Ritalin family. Patricia, let's dance this song out there and I'll tell you my secret.

Patricia Oh, right.

Tyler Billy has a secret?

Billy Not for long, of *course*!

Giggling, **Billy** *pulls* **Patricia** *into the other room, off.* **Stephen** *looks at Tyler.*

Stephen Hey, you.

Tyler 'What's up, man.'

Stephen 'Not much, dude.'

Tyler 'Cool party.'

Stephen 'Thanks.'

Tyler   'What's your name?'

Stephen   'I'm Stephen.'

Tyler   'Hey, what's up, I'm Tyler.'

Stephen   'Would you like to dance, Tyler?'

Tyler   'Umm . . . I actually have to go home right now and wash my hair.'

Stephen   'Oh, right. Okay.'

Stephen gets up and mock-walks away. Tyler mock-rises.

Tyler   'But . . . I have time for one dance.'

Stephen *turns. They break the joke. They begin dancing.*

So when everyone leaves tonight . . . can we take a bath together?

Stephen   Yes.

Tyler   Yay!

Stephen   I don't know how clean the tub/is.

Billy *enters.*

Billy   Patricia's boyfriend is *hot*!

Stephen *and* **Tyler** *turn and stop dancing.*

Stephen   Yeah, he's really/beautiful.

Tyler   Does anybody need a drink?

Stephen   I'm/fine.

Billy   No.

Tyler *goes. Pause.*

Stephen   So – um – I know, Tyler, you know, tells me you're a musical-theatre actor – what is it like for musical-theatre actors? It must be tough, there aren't that many roles for younger people, right?

Billy   Well, there's chorus.

Stephen   Right.

Billy   So . . . there's someone here that I've *slept* with – I think. Except I'm not sure he remembers me – also, *I* have a *wee* bit of a memory problem?

Stephen   Yeah?

Billy   It was a few years ago, I'm pretty sure it's him. He had, like – (*he measures out his hands*) and I was like, um, hel-*lo*. Would you like me to *wrap* that for you? I think his name's Donald – such a bad name – but anyway, I sent Patricia on a mission to talk to him and find out his name. I'm *pretty* sure it's him.

Stephen   Wow.

Billy   So, I'd love to read your work.

Stephen   Really? Oh, sure.

Billy   Yeah, Tyler says it's so beautiful.

Stephen   Wow. Yeah, I'd be more/than happy –

Tyler *and* **Patricia** *enter,* **Tyler** *with drink.*

Billy   Patricia! Did you find out?

Patricia   His name is Philip.

Billy   Philip? Oh – Does anyone want, I really want cocaine. Why does nobody have any here? It doesn't make/sense.

Stephen   I guess my friends/aren't –

Patricia   There's a lot of people I don't know/here.

Stephen   I/know.

Billy   Oh – what about that guy? Tyler, you were telling me about some/guy.

Patricia (*to* **Stephen**)   Do you have that book you were telling me about?

Stephen   What/book?

Billy (*to* **Tyler**)   In the building?

Patricia   You were telling me about/some book.

Billy   The guy in/the building, on the floor.

Stephen   Right,/yeah.

Tyler   What guy?

Billy (*to* **Stephen**)   Stephen, there's some guy in your building who sells cocaine. On your floor.

Stephen   Oh.

Pause.

Tyler   I never said it was/cocaine.

Stephen   Yeah, I don't know/what he –

Billy   Well, what else would it be?

Pause.

Why don't we do that?

Stephen   Um – I don't think that's a good idea.

Billy   What apartment is he in?

Stephen   I think – I assume there's some system – I don't think you can just knock on the door.

Billy (*laughing*)   He knocks on your door all the time. What apartment is it?

Stephen   I don't, I don't really feel comfortable, um – with his knowing that someone had come from this apartment . . .

Billy   But Tyler said you were, like, friends with him.

Tyler   I didn't say they were/friends.

Stephen   I basically have interactions with the father,/not –

Patricia   Maybe someone will show up with cocaine.

Pause.

Billy What's amazing to me/is –

Tyler I'm gonna pee.

Tyler *goes off.*

Billy What's amazing to me is that Tyler said they're also on *welfare*? That makes me, like, so angry. I had this actor friend whose father is a millionaire and who gave him money, but this kid, when his acting job ended, he went on unemployment, even though his father was sending him cash. – I mean, how much money, if he's dealing drugs,/how much –

Stephen I don't think the kid – the one's who's dealing/drugs –

Tyler returns.

Tyler People are having sex in your bathroom. They forgot to lock the door, I/just walked –

Billy I'm sure they didn't forget, everyone in this city is an/exhibitionist.

Stephen Who here would be having – I don't/like that.

Billy Were they hot?

Tyler I shut the door really quickly.

Stephen Let me – knock on the door and hurry them up.

Stephen goes, off. Pause.

Patricia I'm gonna check in with Frank.

Billy He is *hot*. Patricia!

Patricia *smiles politely and goes, off.* **Billy** *dances.* **Tyler** *doesn't.*

Billy What?

Tyler Billy – now he knows I was talking about him.

Billy Who?

Tyler Stephen – that I was talking to you about his neighbour.

Billy   That you told me about his little project? His 'help the poor by handing out cigarettes' project?

Tyler   Can we just not bring it up again?

Billy   I'm sorry, I didn't mean to screw anything up. I just wanted some/blow.

Stephen *enters.*

Stephen   'The bathroom has been liberated by the forces of good.'

Tyler   Yay!

Tyler *exits, off. Pause.*

Stephen   So . . . the guy turned out to be not the guy, huh?

Billy   That's the thing – 'Donald', 'Philip'. That's sort of the same name, in a way, it might be him. I guess there's only one way to find out.

(*They laugh.*)

So . . . you've had a lot of contact with the drug dealer?

Stephen   No – no, mostly with his father.

Billy   The crippled guy.

Stephen   Yeah, the – disabled guy, right. Yeah, and – it's not – I'm not sure how much Tyler told you but – it's not the kid who's on welfare. He's not collecting money – it's/ the father.

Tyler *enters.*

Tyler   Now someone else is in there and I knocked and they were like, 'It's gonna take a while.'

Billy   But that's so sick, though.

Stephen   What is?

Billy   That on top of the drug money they're collecting/ welfare.

Stephen   No – I don't think the son gives the father any money – is what I'm saying.

Tyler *looks away.*

Billy (*to* **Tyler**)   Stephen was just telling me some more about the neighbors.

Tyler   Oh.

Stephen   Just – I think it's/complicated.

Patricia *enters.*

Billy   Well, thank God that welfare bill passed so that kind of stuff can't happen as much anymore, thank God.

Patricia   Those boys doing Adderall are nuts, they asked me if I wanted to play strip poker.

Tyler   Really? Oh God –

Stephen (*to* **Billy**)   – No. No, actually – in this building alone – in the apartments no bigger than this one, there are people – families of *ten* living together, three generations.

Stephen *looks to* **Patricia**

Billy   Well, that's what they get, though. They had five years to get off welfare and find/jobs.

Stephen   Are you – do you have any idea about what you're talking/about?

Tyler   – Don't.

Billy   Actually, I/do.

Tyler   Stephen.

Stephen   What?

Pause.

Patricia   Does anyone need a drink?

No one really responds. **Patricia** *goes, off.* **Stephen** *watches her go.*

Billy   I grew up poor.

Stephen *looks back to* **Billy**.

Stephen   Right. Poor, what – what's your/definition?

Billy   And we never went on welfare. My father worked two jobs.

Stephen   I hear that, definitely, but what – what does poor mean to you?

Billy   What do you mean? We were *poor*?

Stephen   Right. Okay. But – the welfare bill has actually been a disaster, you know. You know, the effects are not always visible, they're never immediately apparent, and it coincided with a bright time for what's really a very fragile/economy.

Billy   But it made the poor take responsibility for themselves.

Stephen   This city,/what –

Tyler   Stephen.

Stephen   – What happened in this/city –

Billy   This city is *so* much better than it was even five years ago.

Stephen   Okay, do you really want to have a conversation about this?

Billy   There's less homeless,/there's –

Stephen   You *see* them less – where *you* live –

Billy   – It put a stop to all those welfare mothers who kept having/babies –

Stephen   Welfare – do you – *welfare*/mothers?

Tyler   Stephen.

Stephen   – Why do you keep saying my name?

Tyler   Just . . .

Stephen *turns to* **Billy**.

Stephen I'm happy to have a reasonable conversation with you, I'd like to – but you're not responding to what I'm saying, you're just – you're just saying things.

Pause.

Billy My mother and father worked so hard for me. They gave up their lives for me. No one handed them anything.

Stephen Right. Well – perhaps it was easier for them because they were white.

Billy Excuse me? Would you like me to talk about the anti-Semitism that they/faced all –

Stephen I'm not – being Jewish is very different from being black.

Billy You don't know my life.

Stephen I never said I did.

Billy Yes, you're talking about my life – 'It was easier for them because they were white' –

Stephen Well – I'm – talking about facts of history, facts of race, facts/of –

Billy You don't know my life or their/lives.

Stephen I didn't say/I knew –

Billy My mother is dead.

Stephen We're not talking about that.

Pause. **Billy** *moves to leave the room.*

No – I mean – of course – I'm sure your parents did work hard, I'm sure they encountered anti-Semitism. But – there are not jobs for everyone, particularly not for people who don't speak English well, who weren't given access to a good education, or, I mean – you can't really argue that Jews have had anywhere *near* the experience that blacks have had/in America.

Billy You don't know their/lives, Jesus,

Stephen I'm – no, listen – just – stop being so defensive and listen a/second.

Billy I/am.

Stephen A culture of poverty and racism breeds a – certain social – I mean, can't you, as a gay man, I mean, can't you identify with/other groups?

Billy You just can't expect the world to give you things, that's all I'm saying. No one ever gave me anything. And say what you will about Giuliani, fuck him for shutting down the clubs and all that, and fuck him for trying to censor art, but he cleaned this city up.

Pause.

Stephen It's apartment 6C.

Billy What is?

Tyler Stephen.

Stephen If you want to buy drugs. Apartment 6C.

Pause. **Billy** *looks at* **Tyler**. **Billy** *goes, off. Pause.* **Stephen** *looks at* **Tyler**, *who looks at the floor.*

What? Let him go – let him get punched in the face – fucking privilege, fucking – I'm sorry, Tyler, if someone is going to stand in my apartment and say/racist –

Patricia *enters.*

Patricia Hey.

Stephen Hey.

Patricia So, Frank wants to go home, I have a lot of work to catch up on, so. . .

Stephen Oh.

Patricia I'll talk to you tomorrow. Bye, Tyler.

Tyler Bye, Patricia.

Patricia *goes, off. Pause.*

Tyler (*quietly*)   You should let people have their opinions, Stephen.

Stephen   Not – not when they're racist and/wrong.

Tyler   It's not racist to think welfare is bad, or, or, that all the problems of the world won't be solved if the government gives poor people more money.

Stephen   Tyler, people are/dying.

Tyler   I just want you two to get/along.

Stephen   People are dying in this building. They are dying of poverty, of drugs, I see them every day, there are no jobs, I see their children, they go to schools that are falling/apart.

Tyler *goes to* **Stephen** *and puts his hand on his shoulder.*

Tyler   Fine, but why does it upset you so much?

Stephen   I *live* here!

Tyler   Whoa. Calm down. Shhh.

Pause. **Tyler** *hugs* **Stephen***. They begin dancing slowly.*

Lights rise on **Timothy***'s apartment.* **Shed** *stands, holding the cocaine and the cash.* **Billy** *knocks on his door. Pause.* **Shed** *goes to the door, looks in the peephole. He puts the money and the cocaine in his pockets and opens the door.*

Billy   Hey . . . I'm from across the hall? At the party?

He takes out forty dollars.

I have forty dollars. Do you have any coke?

Pause. **Shed** *looks at him. He lets go the door.* **Billy** *holds the door open, steps inside.* **Shed** *turns around. He takes the forty dollars from* **Billy***, gets cocaine, gives it to* **Billy***.*

Billy   Thanks.

Billy *goes, off.* **Timothy** *enters.*

Timothy   Who was that?

Shed *doesn't answer.*

Timothy   Where's Lily? She go?

Shed   Yes.

Timothy   She go with Dave?

Shed   You a fucking eavesdropper now?

Timothy   Don't worry about that – she's crazy, Shed –

Shed   – I don't care about that –

Timothy   – Don't pay her no mind –

Shed   – Leave me alone –

Timothy   – I'm just saying – she tried to grab my dick once – she's/crazy.

Shed *rushes* **Timothy** *and throws him against the wall. He punches him in the shoulder.* **Timothy** *falls.*

Timothy (*crying out*)   Ahhh! My leg!

Shed *sits down on the couch and turns on the television.* **Timothy** *whimpers a bit, struggles to reach his crutches.*

Billy *enters the bedroom where* **Stephen** *and* **Tyler** *dance.*

Billy   Can we make up, Stephen?

Pause. **Stephen** *looks at* **Billy.**

In **Timothy**'s *apartment, apropos of nothing, from the couch, with anger:*

Shed   Why you gotta all be in people's shit – why you gotta be here all –

Shed *stops himself, turns away.* **Timothy** *reaches his crutches.*

Stephen   Yeah, I don't – I didn't want to fight.

Billy   Me too. I'm sorry if what I said offended you.

Stephen   Don't worry about it.

Billy   Okay.

Pause.

Could you apologize to me too?

Stephen   – Excuse me?

Tyler *turns away.*

Billy   For assuming you knew about my life.

Timothy *struggles to his feet.* **Shed** *turns on video game, plays.*

Stephen   Okay, I just. I think it's important that people –
think about – other people, you know. Think about/what
they –

Billy*'s cellphone rings. He checks it but does not answer. Pause.*
Stephen *looks at* **Tyler.**

Stephen (*flippantly*)   I apologize.

Billy   I accept. Now we can party? Tyler loves you, I want
us to get along. He loves both of us so we should try to at least
like each other.

Stephen   – Right.

Pause.

Billy (*sing-songy*)   I got *blo-ow*!

Billy *takes out cocaine. He scoops some on to a key and sniffs it. He
offers it to* **Tyler**.

Tyler   A little . . .

Tyler *sniffs cocaine.* **Billy** *offers it to* **Stephen**. *Pause.*

Stephen   I'm okay.

Billy   You sure?

Stephen   Yeah, I'm fine.

Billy   It's good, I think.

Billy *puts away the cocaine. Pause.*

Tyler   I'm gonna see if I can pee again.

Tyler *goes, off.*

In **Timothy***'s apartment,* **Timothy** *moves off, in pain.* **Shed** *continues to play video game.*

Billy   So . . . what are you writing these days?

Stephen   I think . . . something just happened.

Billy   No, that's just Tyler being Tyler. He'll be fine, he doesn't like conflict.

Stephen   Why did you do that?

Billy   Do what?

A new song comes on, off. A sound of cheering from the party.

Stephen   You – you brought up – you created/a –

Billy (*starting to dance*)   – I love this song –

Stephen   – Fuck off.

Billy   What? – What is wrong with you?

Pause. **Billy** *goes, off.*

In **Timothy***'s apartment,* **Timothy** *exits, off.* **Shed** *looks back, then turns back to video game. In* **Stephen***'s apartment,* **Tyler** *bounces into the bedroom, dancing.*

Stephen   Hey.

Tyler   What's up, man? Let's dance.

He grabs **Stephen***, tries to dance.* **Stephen** *doesn't dance.*

What's wrong?

Stephen   I'm – upset.

Tyler   Billy's fine, don't worry about it. Come on, dance.

Stephen *dances with* **Tyler** *tentatively. Then stops again.*

Stephen   I don't – it's – *I'm* upset.

Tyler   You're upset.

Stephen   Yeah, I – I'm really sad now.

Pause. **Tyler** *places his hands on* **Stephen**'s *head, and begins making a strange humming sound.* **Stephen** *laughs a little.*

What are you? . . .

Tyler   'I'm using my special powers to take away your pain.' Hmmmmmmmzzz.

Stephen   Oh.

Tyler   I have a call back.

Stephen   For the TV show?

Tyler   Hmmmmmmmzzz.

Stephen *pushes* **Tyler**'s *hands off him.*

Tyler   What?

Stephen   I'm – really sad, Tyler.

Tyler   It's a *party*, Stephen.

Stephen   I know it's –

Tyler *goes to* **Stephen** *and grabs his hand.*

Tyler   Let's go out to the party, come/on.

Stephen (*taking back hand*)   In – a minute.

Long pause. **Stephen** *and* **Tyler** *look at each other.*

Tyler   Fine.

Stephen *doesn't respond. Pause.* **Tyler** *goes off. Pause.* **Stephen** *moves towards party, stops himself.* **Shed** *continues to play the video game, with growing intensity.*

Scene Three

Slide reads: August 3, 2001

Stephen *and* **Patricia** *sit in* **Stephen***'s living room.*

Patricia I always wondered why gay men had all these friends in the way they do. It's so clear. It's so they can separate their sexual and emotional needs, because they're frightened to combine them. Boyfriends who don't have sex, sex without having to have a boyfriend.

Stephen Yeah . . . I dunno. Maybe he'll change his mind. Just – like that. I just . . .

Patricia I'm really sorry.

Pause.

I should get going. Did you have that book? . . .

Stephen Oh, right.

Stephen *gets book, gives it to* **Patricia**. *She looks at it.*

Patricia *On The Edge of the New Century*. There's a title for you.

Stephen It's really great.

Patricia *rises;* **Stephen** *follows. She moves to the door.*

Patricia You know, anyone who's friends with that guy – 'Billy' – all he would talk to me about was how attractive Frank was. And about – whoever this guy was he thought he had had sex with. He was actually why we left.

Stephen Billy?

Patricia Yeah.

Stephen But you said you left because Frank wanted to go. Because you had work to do.

Pause

Patricia Yeah – I mean – we were just being polite.

(*Laughs.*) I felt like I was at work – except instead of a straight guy telling me how attractive I am, it was a gay man telling me how attractive my boyfriend is.

Stephen   Why were you being polite? You weren't at work.

Pause.

Patricia   What do you mean?

Stephen   I thought you left because of Frank – but you're saying you were offended by Billy.

Patricia   Yeah.

Stephen   But you didn't say anything.

Patricia   About what?

Pause.

Stephen   I'm sorry, I'm just . . . I'm really angry.

Patricia   Well – of course you're angry. Tyler said he loved you. He was supposed to love you. He didn't love/you.

Stephen   No. Not that.

Patricia   What?

Stephen   You know – . . .

Pause

You're talking about how you left and. You know, I – I had no support. No one – and this always happens – in these situations, in groups – where the pathological person is validated while the person who is right is somehow made to be ridiculous.

Pause.

Patricia   I see. I think – you're talking about the discussion about/welfare.

Stephen   Yes, when you left. Because I was thinking – I knew that you agreed with me. I knew that, and now you're saying on top of that you were offended by Billy, but you just –

Patricia   Right. Okay. What I was thinking was, was that nobody's mind was going to be changed. Clearly. And it was a ridiculous conversation to be having.

Stephen   It wasn't a ridiculous conversation to be having.

Patricia   No – but at a party. And that guy wasn't going to budge an/inch.

Stephen   But – you know, maybe if you had spoken up – maybe he could have been made to listen. If I had had some support – but, you know, I seemed/like –

Patricia   That never would have happened, that/guy –

Stephen   But you're not seeing how – how I was made to look like a jerk, while Billy gets to – and in front of Tyler, you know, I seem like the asshole.

Pause.

Patricia   I see now. You're feeling that maybe Tyler left you because of this conversation about welfare?

Stephen   Where I looked like an/asshole.

Patricia   Right, but – I think the timing's fortuitous. I don't think it makes sense to say that this one moment – what did he say? 'Different places' – 'need to be alone' – clichés, they mean nothing. So of course you're searching for why, and it was at that moment that you felt Tyler pull away, but . . . But it's not just – it's not – here's what I think happened in that moment – because it was more than just that moment, I mean: you were angry at Tyler for validating Billy because you found Billy offensive, because of how he looked at the world. And you wanted Tyler to look at the world like you do. You could sense that Billy was engaging you in a way meant to humiliate you and test loyalties and yet you couldn't censor/yourself.

Stephen   But now you are implying a psychodrama. You are implying that politics isn't real, that a political discussion is merely a psychodrama. As if what we were talking about isn't valid – as if it's something/else.

Patricia   That's not,/no –

Stephen   Which allows you to leave. To pretend it's
something else and to leave, so I'm left there. The way I look
at the world, alone, unsupported, ridiculous, when I
know/you –

Patricia   You're making this too easy, Stephen.

Stephen   No. That's what you did. You made it easy for
yourself and easy for Billy, you left. You were invisible. You
made yourself invisible.

Patricia   Okay . . . you're – very angry at me.

Stephen   I – am. Yeah. Yeah, if you had supported me,
Tyler might have seen that I wasn't – Billy might have listened
and Tyler would have – fuck it, whatever. You can go.

Patricia   Well – now I don't want to go.

Stephen   Well, I want you to.

Pause. **Patricia** *moves to the door.*

No one's mind can be changed. This is the world.

Patricia *stops, turns.*

Patricia   Would you like me to go?

Stephen   Let everyone have their own opinions, everyone's
opinion is equal, everyone/is valid.

Patricia   Maybe you need to change the way you talk to
people who don't agree with you. Maybe that's what Tyler
saw – that you/weren't –

Stephen   Oh?

Patricia   Yeah. Maybe you need to change the way you talk
to people you feel superior/to.

Stephen   Blah blah blah. Just go.

Pause. **Patricia** *goes to the table, places the book down, and leaves, off.*
Pause. **Stephen** *lights a cigarette. A knock on the door.*

Hello?

Timothy's voice   Hey, sorry to bother you, you got a cigarette?

Pause.

Stephen   I quit.

Timothy's voice   What's that?

Stephen   I QUIT.

As I wend the shores I know not,
As I listen to the dirge, the voices of men and women wrecked,
As I inhale the impalpable breezes that set in upon me,
As the ocean so mysterious rolls toward me closer and closer,
At once I find, the least thing that belongs to me, or that I see
    or touch, I know not,
I, too, but signify, at the utmost, a little washed-up drift,
A few sands and dead leaves to gather,
Gather, and merge, myself as part of the sands and drift.

                    – Walt Whitman, from 'Elemental Drifts'

Act Three

Scene One

Slide reads: September 27, 2001

Timothy's *apartment.* **Lily** *sits across from* **Timothy**. *They are drinking beer and smoking.* **Timothy** *has a prosthetic leg. Lily looks at a photo album.*

Timothy   I was married twenty years. Lived here the whole time . . .

Lily   Wow. That's true love.

Timothy   True love, I don't know about that . . .

Lily (*re: picture*)   Look at you. (*Beat.*) I've never known true love, I've known passion.

Timothy   I don't know if you would call it true love.

Lily   No, you loved each other. Look at that. I've only known passion.

Timothy   I have memories.

Lily *flips through photos.*

Timothy   You wouldn't say we got along usually. There was a time we partied all the time and that wasn't good. There's nothing you can do when certain things happen. You can wait for them to be over. Looking back. You wouldn't say we had a good marriage. But you look back. It's strange. I do wonder why God let me live.

Pause.

You party a lot?

Lily   I don't know, depends.

Timothy   Yeah. I did lots of things there was no need to do. We wasted a lot of years. I drove trucks. I was gone a lot. We partied together, we partied a lot. Then before you knew it I would go away. She would still party . . . then the accident . . .

Lily   What happened? Shed never said.

Lily *hands photo album back to* **Timothy.**

Timothy   He never told you?

Lily   Not really.

Timothy   We went out to dinner. I was driving back. We had wine. I just drove wrong.

Pause. She looks at him.

I was trying to pass a car that was going so slow – my God, so slow. I was tired. I wasn't working, we were talking about that. I was telling her we had to figure something out. Shed's been paying the rent here. I'd like to work again. It was an old lady – she was driving so slow. I misjudged it. I drove my whole life. You get cocky.

Lily   Did you know she was dead?

Timothy   My leg was bleeding very bad. I looked at her and she was dead.

Pause. **Timothy** *opens the photo album and looks.*

Lily   It was true love.

Timothy   You think back. There's probably nothing in my future. Stupid leg.

Lily   But you have your leg now.

Timothy   You can tell. I still limp. The color is wrong.

Lily   I've never had true love. At least you've had that.

Timothy   I don't know . . .

Lily   It was true love.

Timothy *focuses on one photo.*

Timothy   It was true love.

Pause.

You gonna watch TV?

Lily   No.

Timothy   Yeah. Well, I'm going to sleep.

Timothy *rises.*

Lily   Where is he?

Timothy   He usually is home now. I don't know.

Lily   Where is he?

Timothy   I don't know. Good night. I guess I won't see you again.

Lily   Did he miss me? Did he ever say he missed me?

Timothy   Oh. You know. Shed don't talk. But I'm sure he did. You were here a lot, and no one was here, he stopped having anyone here.

Lily   Really?

Timothy   Sure, yeah. It was just you.

Lily   He probably didn't miss me, though.

Timothy   I don't know. He's a kid, so he don't have to think, you know?

Pause. **Lily** *rises and hugs* **Timothy**. *She releases.*

Timothy   Good night.

Lily   When you get a new lady, you send me a postcard so I can say, 'I told you so! I told you you're a big sexy man!'

Timothy   Ha, I don't know about that! We'll see!

Timothy *goes, off. Pause.* **Lily** *begins to breathe quickly, as if having a panic attack. She turns on the television. She lights a cigarette. She gets up and begins to pace. She begins scratching her arm furiously.*

The sound of a key in the door. **Lily** *stops, turns.* **Shed** *enters, wearing a face mask.*

Lily Hey.

Shed *takes off his face mask.*

Lily Smell getting to you.

Shed *crosses to the couch, puts down his backpack.*

Shed Bad tonight.

Pause.

Lily Been a while.

Shed What's up?

Lily You doing good?

Shed *shrugs. Pause.*

Lily You got a job, I heard!

Shed *nods.*

Lily I'm – going home, I'm going back, so . . . I'm leaving tomorrow, I wanted to say goodbye . . .

Shed You going home.

Lily Yeah. – Dave says hi.

Shed Dave says hi.

Lily Yeah. He misses you, he says.

Shed Uh-huh.

Lily He says you don't answer the phone anymore.

Shed Got rid of it.

Pause.

Lily He says he came here, he says you don't answer the door either.

Shed Don't answer the door, no.

Lily You sent him his money in the mail?

Shed Yup.

Lily   Wow.

Pause.

So I didn't know if you were okay, or . . .

Shed   Fine.

Lily   You didn't miss much. Dave's back with Maryanne. He stays in his room, doesn't leave the apartment, he bought all these gas masks and night-vision goggles. Tell me about your job, it sounds brilliant.

Shed   It's good.

Lily   It's a fancy hotel?

Shed   Yeah.

Lily   How'd you get it?

Shed   Looked right, I guess.

Lily   When did you start?

Shed   End of August.

Lily   What's it like, you like it?

Shed   Beautiful. It's this guy, Ian Schrager. He has a shitload of hotels. This one, you go in there, it's like the world don't exist. It's like, you got a escalator. Lime-green light. You go up, it's all dark, there's big plants everywhere, like, growing out the walls. Huge chandeliers, like. It's so cool, it's got, like, special effects – like those 3D things, holograms and shit. Everybody wear a uniform, like. Beautiful women waitresses. Outdoor courtyard, trees, big chairs. Matt Damon's having his birthday party there in a couple of weeks, they got famous people all the time in there, go there.

Lily   Wow. I love Matt Damon.

Shed   Pay's fine. Lot of coke there, everybody look like they on it. What people pay for cigarettes, what they pay for drinks, damn . . .

Pause.

Lily   I miss you. I got all wrapped up with Dave, then, I partied a lot . . .

Pause.

Shed   Why you going?

Lily   I dunno. I miss it. It's a nice time to go back, the autumn.

Pause.

Yeah. I got you – I wanted to give you something to remind you of me.

She reaches into her pocket and pulls out a photo-booth photograph. She hands it to him.

Three pictures of me. The first one is the crazy me, see. The second one is the sad me. The third one is the real me, no expression.

Shed *looks at the photograph.*

Lily   I was thinking of lifting my top for the last one, but, you know, it was in the arcade, I felt weird.

Pause.

Shed   Thanks.

Lily   Plus, you don't know where those pictures end up, if they stay in the computer or whatever. Don't want my tits all over the place, even if I do have nice tits.

Lily *laughs.*

Shed   I don't see too much difference between crazy you and sad you.

Lily   The third one is the real me, no expression. I think I might miss you the most, you know.

Shed   Yeah?

Lily   I don't know why. I don't know. I'm clean for four days.

Pause.

Shed   That's really good.

Lily   Four days. I'm going crazy. I got some Xanax but I took it all. Nightmares. So. Yeah.

Pause.

I'm gonna go. But you gotta give me something before I go.

Shed   What?

Lily   Something to remember you by. I gave you my picture, now you gotta give me something.

Pause. **Shed** *looks around.*

Shed   Don't know what I got.

Pause. **Shed** *looks at her. She moves to him and hugs him hard. He hugs her back. Pause. She reaches down to his crotch.*

Lily   I knew it!

She laughs. Pause. She moves her hand on his crotch. Pause. **Shed** *removes his shirt. They embrace.*

Scene Two

A bar. Loud music. **Stephen** *stands alone.* **Leo** *approaches. Pause.*

Leo   YOU LOOK FAMILIAR.

Stephen   WHAT?

Leo   YOU LOOK FAMILIAR.

Stephen   I DO?

Leo   HAVEN'T WE MET?

Stephen   I DON'T THINK SO.

Leo   I DON'T KNOW WHY I THINK SO. ARE YOU HERE ALONE?

Stephen   YEAH.

Leo   WHY DO I THINK I KNOW YOU? DO YOU
COME HERE A LOT?

Stephen   NO.

Leo   WHY NOT?

Stephen   WHEN I HAD A BOYFRIEND, I DIDN'T GO
OUT.

Leo   WHEN DID YOU BREAK UP?

Stephen   A WHILE AGO.

Leo   WHAT'S A WHILE?

Stephen   FEELS LIKE LONGER THAN IT'S BEEN,
PROBABLY.

Leo   YOU MISS HIM?

Stephen   YEAH.

Leo   YOU WERE IN LOVE?

Stephen   YES.

Leo   WHAT HAPPENED?

Stephen   I DON'T KNOW. HE BROKE UP WITH
ME.

Leo   WHY?

Stephen   WHY DO PEOPLE BREAK UP WITH
PEOPLE?

Leo   YOU DON'T WANT TO TALK ABOUT IT?

Stephen   NOT PARTICULARLY.

Leo   WHERE DO YOU LIVE?

Stephen   NEAR HERE.

Pause.

Leo   DO YOU WANT TO GO THERE?

Scene Three

Stephen's *bedroom*. **Stephen** and **Leo** *enter*.

Leo   I'm serious, it makes perfect sense. This was Giuliani's greatest fantasy and his greatest fear. He's always had a fascist impulse, which this fits perfectly. But, remember, he had prostate cancer, and there was all that media coverage about how he might be impotent. Months later, the two tallest, most phallic buildings in New York City go down. What was happening in his body, happening in his city.

Stephen   Huh. That's really interesting.

Leo *takes out cocaine, does a bump.* **Leo** *gives* **Stephen** *cocaine.* **Stephen** *sniffs cocaine.*

Leo   What's funniest is he's just *like* the Taliban – obsessed with forcing his rules, his ideology, violently upon the people: close down the clubs where gays congregate, shut down the strip clubs where women reveal their bodies, cancel funding for art museums who show art that subverts his religious beliefs: he probably *deeply* identifies with the Taliban.

Stephen   Right . . .

Leo   – Is this the window?

Stephen   That's the window.

Leo *looks out the window. Long pause. The sound of a fighter jet passing.*

Leo   The F-14s are flying low tonight.

He turns to **Stephen.**

(*brightly*) So. What are we going to do now that we've moved out of a public space and into a private one?

Stephen (*smiling*)   Have sex.

Leo *laughs. He looks around and finds a photograph.*

Leo   Is this your boyfriend?

Stephen   Ex. Yeah.

Leo   What was his name?

Stephen   Why do you want to know?

Leo   I dunno.

Stephen   Tyler. I'm gonna brush my teeth.

Leo   Okay.

Stephen *exits, off.* **Leo** *stares at the photograph. Then he puts it down and takes off his shoes.* **Stephen** *enters.*

Stephen   Hey.

Leo   Hey. Have you heard from him since the eleventh?

Stephen   Who?

Leo   Tyler.

Stephen   No . . .

Leo   No?

Stephen   Nope.

Leo   I don't believe in love.

Stephen   You don't?

Leo   No, I think it's a vague word that is applied indiscriminately.

Stephen (*laughs*)   Oh.

Leo   To me, a more interesting question is what people are doing to each other in each other's company under the guise of 'love'.

Stephen   What do you mean?

Leo   Like – what is love? What *is* it? I mean, you can say, okay – okay, this person fucks me, he calls me, he eats meals with me, he tells me about his day, I am in his thoughts and fantasies, I do things and he has feelings about them – you can make a list of facts. But what makes those facts love? What?

And – I couldn't figure it out. So I decided there was no such thing. And I was fine with that.

Stephen   Uh-huh

Leo   The idea of love is so heteronormative, and it's perfect for capitalism: it prevents people from thinking about real problems in their lives, it makes them think, when they feel bad, that something is wrong with them and not the world, it makes people form families and buy things for those families. Love's the new religion, and I'm agnostic.

He begins removing his clothes.

You're so adorable.

Stephen   You too.

Stephen *turns out the light.* **Leo** *approaches him. We can barely see them. They undress and embrace.*

Leo   Put on some music.

He gets in bed. **Stephen** *puts music on – R & B. He gets into bed.* **Leo** *begins to fellate* **Stephen***, then kisses him.* **Leo** *gets on top of* **Stephen** *and begins moving.*

Mmm.

Stephen   That feels good.

Leo   You like that?

Stephen   Yeah.

Leo *continues.* **Stephen** *turns him over and gets on top of him and kisses him.*

Leo   You can kiss.

Stephen (*laughs*)   I can?

Leo   Mm-hmm.

They kiss. **Leo** *wraps his legs around* **Stephen***. Then* **Leo** *takes his own hands and put them behind his head. He takes Stephen's right hand and clasps it to his two hands, as if to restrain them.*

Harder.

Stephen *thrusts against* **Leo** *harder. Then* **Leo** *eases* **Stephen** *off him.* **Leo** *gets on his hands and knees.*

Leo (*sweetly*)   Rub against me like you're fucking me.

Stephen *does.*

Leo   That's good. Mm.

He masturbates himself as **Stephen** *rubs against him from behind.*

Mmmm.

Stephen   Uh. Uh. Uhmm.

Leo   You can get rougher.

Stephen   Rougher?

Leo   Yeah.

Stephen *moves a bit more roughly.* **Leo** *takes* **Stephen**'s *hand, puts it on his breast, squeezes his hand around it.*

Leo   Like that. Mmmm. Make sure you tell me if you think you're gonna come.

Stephen   Okay.

He continues.

Uh. Uh. Uhmm. Uh. Uh./Uhmm

Leo   Mmm. Rougher

Stephen   Rougher?

Stephen *moves more roughly.* **Leo** *takes* **Stephen**'s *hand from his breast, puts it on top of his head.*

Leo   Pull on my hair a little.

Stephen *does. He arches his neck, kisses* **Leo**.

Leo   Yes – harder. Mmmm.

Distant sound of fighter jet overhead.

Harder.

Sound of fighter jet fades. **Stephen** *becomes more aggressive.*

Yes, *more.* Mmmm.

Stephen   Uhhh. Uhhhh.

Stephen *rubs more roughly. This goes on a while.*

Leo   Mm. You're fine, right?

Stephen   What?

Leo   I'm fine – we're both fine – you don't have – you don't have/HIV.

Stephen   No.

Leo   *More.* Oh God.

Stephen *continues, getting rougher.*

Stephen   You like that?

Leo   Yes.

Stephen   Yeah? You like that?

Leo   Yes. Fuck me.

Stephen   Yeah, you want me to fuck you?

Leo   Yes please.

Stephen   Yeah?

Leo   I like it.

Stephen   I like it too. Uh. Uh.

Leo   Go inside me.

Stephen   Yeah?

Leo   You can go inside me.

Stephen (*stopping for a moment*)   Wait – go? – literally?

Leo   Keep – it's okay if you hurt me. Keep going.

Stephen   I –

Leo   Please fuck me.

Stephen   I/don't –

Leo   Fuck my pussy.

Pause. Then **Stephen** *enters him, somewhat awkwardly.* **Leo** *grimaces a little.* **Stephen** *fucks him, slow at first, then faster.*

Oh my God . . .Oh God . . .Oh God . . .

Stephen   Yeah.

Leo   *Fuck* my pussy, *fuck* it, oh *God*. Yes –

Stephen *stops.*

Leo   What? Did you come?

Pause. **Stephen** *releases, lays back on the bed.*

Stephen   No . . .

Leo   Why did you stop?

Stephen   I'm sorry.

Pause. **Leo** *grabs* **Stephen***'s penis and begins to masturbate him.*

Leo   Are you close to coming?

Stephen   I . . .

Leo   Come on my face.

Leo *puts his face near* **Stephen***'s penis and masturbates it while masturbating himself.* **Stephen** *puts his hand on* **Leo***'s hand, stops him.*

Stephen   I'm sorry, I have to stop.

Pause. **Leo** *lays back, masturbates himself. This takes a while.* **Stephen** *watches him a bit, then looks around his room. Finally* **Leo** *orgasms.*

Leo   Uhhhhh –

Pause.

Stephen   Let me get you a towel.

He gets **Leo** *a towel and gives it to him.* **Leo** *cleans himself.* **Stephen** *turns off music and dresses.* **Leo** *puts the towel on the floor and dresses. As they do this:*

That was interesting, the comparisons you were making before with the Taliban and Giuliani.

Leo   Uh-huh?

Stephen   I've been reading about Afghanistan – the chaos of the region. So many tribes – so many different groups – disconnected, historically, from their/central government.

Leo   Right.

Stephen   Disconnected from their leaders – and disconnected from each other – all these various groups occupying the same space without being able to/find a common –

Leo   Uh-huh.

Stephen   Just – how fractured and isolated they are – like New York, too, in some ways . . .

Pause. **Leo** *and* **Stephen** *are dressed.* **Leo** *looks at* **Stephen**.

Leo   Nice to meet you.

Stephen   You're gonna go?

Leo *smiles.*

Stephen   You don't have to.

Leo   That's okay.

Stephen   Are you sure? I could make some tea . . .

Leo   I'm fine. Bye.

Leo *goes, off.* **Stephen** *sits down on his bed. He looks out of the window.*

Lights rise on **Timothy**'s *apartment.* **Lily** *is at the door with* **Shed**. *They are dressed.*

Lily   Okay. Say a prayer the plane doesn't fly into the Empire State Building.

Shed   Ha. I will.

Lily   Yeah. So . . . . (*Laughs.*) Nice knowing you.

Shed   You too.

Lily   Yeah. Okay.

Pause.

Congrats again on your job, that's really great.

Shed   Yeah . . .

Lily   You're a good guy. Shed. My buddy Shed.

So . . . Anyway.

She starts to go.

Shed   Hold on – it's bad out there – take this.

Shed *hands her his face mask.*

Lily   Oh.

She looks at it a beat.

Shed   Here, I do it.

He stands behind her, puts it over her mouth and nose. She stands, still for a moment, then begins to cry.

Shed   What's wrong now?

Lily   Dunno . . .

Shed   It's okay . . .

Lily   Yeah . . . Okay. Bye.

Shed   Bye.

She goes, off. **Timothy** *enters.*

Timothy   That Lily?

Shed   Yeah.

Timothy   She gone?

Shed   Yeah.

Timothy   Going home.

Shed   Yeah.

Pause.

Timothy   You liked that girl, huh?

Shed   She all right.

Timothy   You liked having her around.

Shed   What you gonna do?

Timothy   How was work?

Shed *sits down, turns on TV.*

Shed   I got laid off.

Timothy   – What?

Shed   Nobody in the hotel. Nobody there, tourists not coming, so, they letting the most recent people go.

Timothy   Oh Christ. You got fired? No!

Shed   And it's like – it's like, I don't understand – what's – w-w-wrong w-with – me –

Shed *starts to cry.*

Timothy   Oh God.

Shed   It's like – I know what not to do, in my life, but I don't know – what *t-t-to* do, you know?

Timothy   No – that's not your fault – people get/fired.

Shed *(fighting tears with anger)*   I don't know what to DO.

Timothy   No – you can't blame things – it's just how things – it's the world.

Pause. **Shed** *cries.* **Shed** *opens his backpack, takes out a carton of cigarettes.*

Shed (*overcoming tears*)   Fucking, you believe people pay ten dollars a pack? In the hotel. If you go on the street, five dollars, ten dollars inside. They fired me, I took some.

Timothy *smiles.*

Timothy   Thank you.

Shed   Not a problem.

Timothy   You'll be okay, you'll/figure –

Shed   Whatever –

Timothy   You'll figure it/out.

Shed   No point, no point talking about it.

Pause.

Timothy   Maybe I can get a job when I'm done with rehab. Then I won't be here so much, I won't be around the house so much. Maybe I can drive again. They say it's a possibility.

Shed *nods.*

Timothy   I know I'm here/a lot –

Shed   Okay, I hear you. Go – go to sleep.

Pause. **Timothy** *walks, off.* **Shed** *reaches for his backpack, looks in, takes out another carton of cigarettes. Gets up, exits, goes to* **Stephen**'s *door, knocks.* **Stephen** *looks. He exits his bedroom and goes to the door.*

Stephen   Hello?

Shed's voice   Hey, it's your neighbour.

Stephen   Yes?

Shed's voice   Got – something for you, 'wanna open up.

Stephen   What?

Shed's voice   I got something for you.

Pause. **Stephen** *opens the door.*

Stephen   Hey, what's up?

Shed *holds out a carton of cigarettes.*

Shed   Hey – just to thank you, got these for you, you know . . .

Stephen   Oh. Thank you.

Stephen *takes the carton. Pause.*

Thanks.

Shed   Yeah.

Stephen   You guys – you guys okay?

Shed   Yeah, we fine.

Stephen   Your dad's okay?

Shed   My dad. Oh. That's not my dad. That's my uncle. But yeah, he's okay.

Stephen   Oh – good.

Shed   He got his leg finally. They finally gave him his leg, so.

Stephen   That's great.

Shed   That's my uncle. He lived there, I lived there with him and my aunt, but she died in the car accident, where he lost his leg. So it's good he got his leg, so.

Stephen   Oh – oh God.

Pause.

Shed   You see it happen?

Stephen   I – I saw it from my bedroom window. I saw the whole thing.

Shed   Yeah. I went up on the roof . . . saw that . . .

Stephen   Terrible.

Shed   Yeah.

Pause.

Anyway. That's it.

Stephen   Thank you.

Shed   You welcome.

Shed *goes.* **Stephen** *shuts the door.*

To write: to refuse to write – to write by way of this refusal . . .

– Maurice Blanchot, *The Writing of the Disaster*

Epilogue

Slide reads: October 9, 2001

The bar. **Patricia** *stands behind the bar. It's empty.* **Stephen** *sits with a soda. An American flag draped behind the bar.*

Patricia   And then he says, 'So I was thinking you and I would have an affair.'

Stephen   Oh God.

Patricia   Sixty-two years old, this man. I'm telling you – visual artists.

Stephen   Painters are so weird . . .

Patricia   What's wrong with them?

Stephen   Aren't they stuck at the anal stage? Isn't paint – isn't it something to do with the child playing with feces? I think I read that in Freud.

Young Businessman 1 *enters, sits at the end of the bar.*

Patricia   Hey there, Howard.

Howard (**Young Businessman 1**)   Hey, Patricia.

Howard *looks up at the television.*

Stephen (*quietly*)   How's he doing?

Patricia   I haven't seen him in a week.

She goes over to **Howard**.

You want a Stella?

Howard   Thank you.

She gets him a beer.

How's business?

Patricia   It's picking up. People still aren't eating out, but they're drinking.

Howard   That's good. I need this beer, Jesus.

Patricia   Yeah? What's going on, is there any news about Ron? Have they found his/body yet?

Howard   They're not gonna find him, it's all just ash, they should give/up.

The bar phone rings. Pause. **Howard** *motions for her to answer.*

Patricia (*picks up*)   Hello?

Howard *turns to* **Stephen**.

Howard   It's weird. I was at the subway, just now . . . The train was late, like five minutes. That happens all the time. But I started getting pissed off. And more and more people started coming down, into the station. And the train kept not coming. Kept looking down the tunnel. Nothing. No announcement. Must have been two, maybe three hundred people on the platform. And I thought – I started getting, like, claustro-phobic.

Patricia *hangs up the phone, listens.*

Howard   And I knew – I knew the train would come. Rationally – I knew – trains are late all the time. But I had this feeling – like something was gonna happen. Even though I knew, I knew the train would come, nothing was wrong, there was just some delay. But it was like – like if I didn't get out of there, something bad was gonna happen. And I left – left the station, walked here.

Stephen   Wow.

Howard   I'm a rational guy. I knew the train was coming but . . . – blah blah blah.

Howard *sips beer. Pause.*

Patricia   Market's doing better.

Howard   Market's fine. – It just doesn't make sense . . . how something that was there goes away . . .

Howard *looks up at the stock ticker on the TV.* **Patricia** *moves to* **Stephen**.

Patricia   What are you doing tonight?

Stephen   I was actually thinking of taking a walk down there. Be a witness. Say that I saw it. I was there. This is what it was like.

On the TV, footage of George Bush, stock ticker running below.

Howard   That's right. Bomb the shit out of them. Go over there and bomb them to the fucking Dark Ages. (*Chanting.*) U-S-A! U-S-A! U-S-A! (*Laughing.*) Come on, Patricia. Show a little patriotism.

Patricia   That's okay, you got enough for both of us.

Howard (*smiling.*)   Yeah, I do, don't I?

He sips his beer. **Patricia** *turns to* **Stephen**. *She smiles at him.*

Stephen   You're so good with these guys, you know that.

Patricia   What else are you gonna be?

Howard   U-S-A! U-S-A!

He raises his beer.

A toast, what do you say?

Beat. **Stephen** *smiles, raises his soda.* **Patricia** *raises a bottle of water.*

To the USA!

Stephen   To where we live.

Patricia   Cheers.

They toast. **Howard** *turns back to TV.* **Patricia** *starts wiping down the bar. Stephen watches her.*